$100M Series: LOST CHAPTERS

*Lost Treasures from
$100M Offers, $100M Leads,
and $100M Money Models*

ALEX HORMOZI

Disclaimer

The information provided in this book is for educational and informational purposes only. The author, publisher, and licensed distributor have made reasonable efforts to ensure that the information within was accurate at the time of publication. The author, publisher, and licensed distributor make no representation or warranties with respect to the merchantability, fitness for a particular purpose, current or continued accuracy or completeness, and reliability of the contents of this book.

The strategies, tips, and tools discussed in this book are the author's personal opinions and are provided as-is. They are intended to provide helpful and informative material on the subjects addressed in this book. Success in any marketing and business endeavors is based on a wide range of factors unique to each individual or business.

Laws are subject to change and may vary by location and jurisdiction. You, as the reader, are encouraged to consult with a professional where appropriate and review the current local laws before implementing any marketing strategies or campaigns.

Earnings and income representations made by the author are aspirational statements only of your potential earnings. The success of the author and others referenced herein, testimonials, and other examples used are exceptional, non-typical results and are not intended to be and are not a guarantee that you or others will achieve the same results. Individual results will always vary and your results will depend entirely on your individual capacity, work ethic, business, skills and experience, level of motivation, diligence in applying the strategies discussed, the economy, the normal and unforeseen risks of doing business, and other factors within or beyond your control.

No guarantee is made that you will achieve any result at all from the ideas in this book. The author, publisher, and licensed distributor disclaim any representations or warranties (express or implied), including, without limitation, those of merchantability, fitness for any particular purpose, current or continued accuracy or completeness, and reliability. Reliance on the information provided is solely at your own risk. As further described herein, the author, publisher, and licensed distributor shall in no event be held liable to you or any party for any direct, indirect, punitive, special, incidental, speculative, or other consequential damages arising directly or indirectly from any use and/or misuse of this book, which is provided "as is", and without warranties.

As always, the advice of a competent legal, tax, accounting, finance, or other professional should be sought and obtained.

Any statements that express or involve discussions with respect to predictions, goals, expectations, beliefs, plans, projections, objectives, assumptions or future events or performance are not statements of historical fact and may be "forward looking statements." Forward looking statements are based on expectations, estimates, and projections at the time the statements are made that involve a number of risks and uncertainties which could cause actual results or events to differ materially from those presently anticipated.

Running a business involves the risk of loss as well as the possibility of profit. All businesses involve risk, and all business decisions remain the responsibility of the individual. The author, Bumble IP, LLC, Acquisition.com, LLC, and their affiliates (collectively referred to herein as the "Company") have not made any guarantees that the strategies outlined in this book will be profitable or beneficial for you or your business, and the Company is not liable for any potential business losses related to these strategies.

Contents

$100M LOST CHAPTERS

Lost Treasures From $100M Offers, $100M Leads, & $100M Money Models

Why lost chapters? Well, I wrote them and I thought they were useful. But, they didn't fit into the other books. Main reason: they'll deepen your knowledge but aren't required to execute the strategies in the $100M Series. That being said, understanding them at a deeper level certainly won't make you poorer. So, that too.

Next important point—<u>this is an unconventional book</u>. This is a compilation of unreleased chapters from the $100M Series. I organized them as logically as I could, but do not expect the same "through line" my other books have. Think of it more as a sampling of different ideas that can be used independently from one another. As such, feel free to skip around and read them in the order that's most useful for you. The core ideas are worth providing because they'll certainly changes a few business owners' lives. And if that's you, then there's hardly anything more valuable that I could provide.

Organization

I split this "assortment of chapters" into an intro chapter and four sections: Sections A through D. They are as follows.

<u>Intro Chapter: Your first Avatar</u>: This is one of the most important chapters I've written. I ended up writing it because I got so many questions about avatar selection *after* I released *$100M Offers*. If I ever write an updated *$100M Offers*, I will incorporate it into the main book. The process I outline in this chapter is **not** a beginner concept. I use the process I outline with every company I advise. It's *that* useful. If you're not sure where to start, start here.

Section A: Attract goes into more detail on how to use Premium, Free, and Discount offers to increase how many people take you up on your thing. I break down each. The pros and cons, and a bunch of examples from my experience. I also share some relevant data I've collected on each type of offer that I think you'll find valuable.

Section B: The Expensive Customer Problem explains the math behind Customer-Financed Acquisition (CFA). This was the last cut I made to *$100M Money Models*. Too many people got bogged down by the math. But, if you like money math, this explains the powerful concept in more detail. It gives you more in-depth examples on how to calculate the three main metrics of acquisition: Lifetime Gross Profit (LTGP), Cost to Acquire a Customer (CAC), and Payback Period (PPD). If your business doesn't fit the examples in the *$100M Money Models* book, or if you just want to see more examples to deepen your knowledge, then this is for you.

Section C: Advanced Offer Stacking gives you more money models that I cut from the original book, as well as a primer on offer stacking with some in-depth examples I cut in one of the later drafts.

Section D: Expanded Employees Stuff is an expanded chapter from *$100M Leads:* "Employees." I cut this because I thought the chapter began to creep out of the scope of getting leads, and into the area of general management. That being said, it is still valuable, just not for the *$100M Leads* book. This chapter is twice the length of the final "Employees" chapter and gets into management and performance. To make sure people actually get you leads when you pay them, and you get a good return on it.

Since the sections and chapters don't have a major through line, I also include a tiny blurb before each chapter explaining why I cut it and how it could help you. I hope you enjoy them as much as I enjoyed writing them for you.

Your First Avatar

"These aren't the droids you're looking for."
– Obi-Wan Kenobi, Star Wars: A New Hope

Lost Chapter Author Note**: *If I could go back in time, I would include this chapter in the $100M Offers book. It's incredibly important for figuring out who your ideal customer is. And no, this isn't yo mama's "find a niche" chapter. This is real, how-you-make-tons-of-money type stuff.*

2019 - I can't remember the month.

The room was cold and dark. Presenters filed on and off stage. We sat at the "cool kids" table for business owners who had software over $10,000,000 ARR (annual recurring revenue). We felt good about ourselves. Our software company ALAN had recently crossed the $1,700,000 per month threshold in its first six months.

As we chatted between speakers, the event host got on stage. "Our next speaker is someone everyone should pay close attention to. This man is responsible for over $50 billion in sales." The noise in the room died down. The host continued, "...He is a specialist in pricing and profit maximization. He worked for years at Vista, one of the most renowned software private equity funds in the world." *Gulp. Reality check. I'm still a minnow.*

The speaker broke down the process Vista used to grow companies. Their method was unlike any I had heard. Here's how it worked.

When they consider acquiring a company, they analyze the company's current customers. They look for the customers who stay the longest and pay the most. Then, they score them according to this value. The highest scores go to the customers worth the most, the lowest to the ones worth the least. If they feel there's a vein of underserved valuable customers, they buy the company.

Once they buy a company, they'd cut channels that brought the low-value customers. Then, they double down on the channels that brought in the best ones.

That's it. More of the high-profit customers. Fewer low-profit customers. Rinse. Repeat.

When he broke down the math, it became even more obvious. It was Pareto's principle (80/20) on steroids. 20% of customers bring in 80% of revenue. If you replace the 80% with those high spenders, you grow the business 5x. No small feat, especially in billion dollar companies. I wondered how I could apply this method across our portfolio. Since then, it's become a pillar of our value acceleration method (VAM) at acquisition.com.

Finding the Right Customers

Earlier, I talked about picking the right market. It's an important strategic business decision. Choosing the perfect avatar is a subset of that larger decision. This is where we become more nuanced about exactly who we serve, and more importantly, *who we do not*.

There are four steps to installing this process. I outline them below. Then, I share what we found after implementing this in Gym Launch. Here are the steps.

1) <u>Survey your customers</u>: Set up a form with the questions below and send it out. Or, for higher engagement, go over it with them live at an event or on a call. Make sure they show they completed it to receive some benefit. Ask them every relevant detail you'd want to know. Here's an example of questions I would ask business services customers:

   a) *Demographics*: Who are they? Age? Gender? Political affiliation? Geographic location? Digital Location? Single/Divorced? Partnered in business or solopreneur?

   b) *Business Stats Before & Current*: Revenue? Profit? # of employees? Churn? Pricing? Products? Customer lifetime value? # of customers? Niche? How long in business?

   c) *Aspirations*: What was their goal upon purchasing your services/products? What problem were they trying to solve?

   d) *Buying Process*: What's the single biggest reason they bought? Was there a trigger event that caused them to buy? Did they consume any specific piece of content? Was there a specific testimonial they consumed? How many pieces did they consume? When did they first hear about you vs. when they bought? Where did they first see us? Did someone refer them?

2) <u>Find your biggest spenders</u>: Sort the replies by the customers you like the most, spent the most, and stayed the longest. Focus on the top 20%. Ignore the rest.

3) <u>See what they have in common</u>: This takes reading through all the answers and using your brain. I know. Thinking is hard. The good news is, your competitors won't do it—easy advantage. Goal: Come up with the fewest qualifiers they all have in common. Now, list them out. Usually there are three to five qualifiers.

4) <u>Execute</u>: Once you have these answers you're going to do two important things.

   a) *Speak to your new avatar.* Be up front about your customer requirements. Get all advertising to speak directly to them. You will repel the bad customers and attract the good ones. Stop selling anyone who does not meet your ideal customer requirements. Seriously, stop it. Then, increase effort on the channels these people come through.

b) *Re-engineer the sales process.* Look at what caused these better customers to buy. Reverse-engineer the buying process your best customers went through. Then, make it happen on purpose.

Pro Tip: You Make More Because of Who They Are, <u>Not</u> Because of Who You Are

The profit you make comes from the premium you can charge for your stuff. The price reflects this premium. You can increase the price if you increase the value. The beauty of selling to better customers means you provide more value for the same work. Let me explain. You can charge more because of who they are, rather than who you are.

<u>Quick Example</u>. Imagine you're a sales page designer. Let's say you improved a sales page to convert from 5% conversion to 7%. As a result, your client makes more money. Let's look at the value you provide two different customers for the same work. If company A made $100,000 per month from the page, they now make $140,000 per month. If company B made $10,000,000 per month, they'd now make $14,000,000 per month. You work the same amount in both cases. But, you provided more value to company B (by a lot). And, you could charge for it. Let's say you charged 10% of growth. For the first business, you'd make $40,000 per year. Not bad. From company B, you'd make $4,000,000 per year. Much better. You gotta think different to make crazy money. Serving the right customer is one of those ways.

Pro Tip: What To Do If You Have No Customers - Start With What You Know

Want to know how the best venture capitalists invest in startups? They pick the founders with past experience relative to the industry they want to serve. This makes sense. There's a lot of in-depth knowledge that takes time to learn. A fast track for new entrepreneurs is to start with the industry you know the most about. Most of us have *some* inside knowledge due to friends, family, past jobs, etc. Even within that subset, you just want to pick the people you can help *the most*. Create a narrow target, then serve them first. Don't get fancy. Start with what you know, then branch out over time as you learn more. You can run the customer analysis process again once you have more customers to survey.

Here's what happened after we did it. We did steps one through three. We surveyed. We sorted for the biggest spenders. Saw what they had in common. Then executed. Please find below the results of this activity on our Gym Launch business.

Findings from Steps 1–3 about our best customers:

<u>Demographics</u>: Right leaning/conservative, married, 25–45, male, gym owner, US-based

<u>Business Requirements</u>: Signed lease, 1+ employees minimum, $10,000+ per month revenue minimum when starting, minimum 30 existing clients

<u>Aspirations</u>: $1M+ gym, not work so much, open more locations

<u>Buying Reasons</u>: Not enough leads, "bad market," bad pricing, can't find good employees

Step 4a: New Redefined Avatar: We surveyed our customers to see what the top 20% had in common. In other words, we got to see what our most successful customers looked like. **Actions:** We focused on the audiences that had the highest concentration of these types of gym owners. We spelled out our requirements in our ads and pages. We talked only about the specific problems and aspirations of our best customers, rather than *all* customers.

Findings from Steps 1–3 about how they bought:

After looking at the data, we found that 78% of our top customers had consumed <u>AT LEAST TWO</u> pieces of long-form content *before* purchasing from us. This means that if we got on the phone with someone who had not done that, our chances of selling them were lower.

Step 4b: Reverse-engineer buying process. Actions: My team then recreated this "ideal" buying experience. From this point onwards, we injected two long-form high-value content pieces to each lead as a part of their buyer journey. And, we increased our total output of content. On top of that, we created a list of our "all-time greatest hits" of content to arm the sales team. They then hand select two to three pieces they think could help the prospect. By doing that, they *forced* them to go through the same buying process that caused our best customers to buy. Note: They were <u>not</u> disguised sales pitches, they were genuinely value-in-advance content. (Like this, hopefully).

A Comparison

A while back, I considered buying an equity stake in a business services company that served fitness business owners. I spent the morning with the business owner learning about his business metrics. From speaking with him, I discovered that despite the owner serving the same vertical as me, *and* making the same number of total sales per month, he was making 70x *less* profit (yes, seventy times less!) Spoiler: it wasn't because we're brilliant. It's because figuring out the most valuable customers to sell to works.

<u>The difference</u>. They accepted anyone with a pulse and a credit card. As a result, they dealt with high customer churn, high costs of acquisition, low retention rates, and lower satisfaction scores. And it had to be that way. Compared to ours, their advice was generic. On the other hand, we selectively pursued and catered to the highest value customers. We ignored all others. This gave us higher retention, higher gross margins, premium pricing, and lots of repeat business. Same market. Different customer segmentation. Monstrously different results. This stuff matters.

Quality > Quantity

Many competitors try to recreate our buyer journey. However, they don't fully commit. They panic, then cut out steps to get more volume. This is often a mistake. In my experience, every time we removed qualification steps, our lead volume increased, but we made less money. Merging marketing and sales into one acquisition department solved this problem for good. Marketing stopped complaining that the sales team wasn't closing. Sales team stopped complaining that they wanted more leads. Everyone came together to focus on what mattered: closing lots of valuable deals. We now use the optimal amount of steps to generate the highest return on advertising *over the long haul.*

Example: I would rather pay $5,000 to acquire $45,000 than pay $1,000 to acquire $5,000 *(even though it costs five times as much).*

Knowing your ideal buyer journey forces patience. You see the business holistically, rather than as a widget to be sold to as many people as possible. The ladder is how small newbie entrepreneurs think—don't think like that.

To give some context, the average Gym Launch competitor has a lifetime gross profit (LTGP) of around $6,000–$8,000. I know because I've looked at buying their businesses. Our LTGP is north of $45,000. Now despite the LTGP being *only* 6–8x higher, the subsequent profits that occur as a result are breathtakingly different. For a moment, I want you to imagine 8x your price, and keeping your costs the same. How much more *profit* would you be making? Probably a lot. That's the difference.

Once you narrow down your focus, you serve fewer customers in the short term. This may mean a short-term decrease in revenue (due to the cost of change). But over the long haul, you get a long term with higher retention and profitability. And unless you're planning on quitting business, why wouldn't you make the right long-term call?

Pro Tip: Sell To People Who Don't Stop Buying

Fortunes are created when we sell things that customers don't stop buying. So our goal should be either to improve our product so everyone wants to keep buying. Or, only sell to customers who historically keep buying. Either solution works. But, this chapter relates only to changing your avatar.

Note: There's a reason companies that have enterprise clients tend to get higher multiples. Reason: they deal with better customers who can afford more, have resources to deploy, and are generally easier to deal with than bottom-feeders. And most importantly, *once they start buying, they tend to continue to buy.*

How to Use This Chapter to Get More High Quality Leads *Immediately*

You have three actions to do at the end of this chapter to get more leads. First, survey your existing customers. Next, use this data to decide which characteristics are leading indicators of high-value customers. Finally, use this information to change your messaging in your advertising, and re-engineer a sales process for them specifically.

Over the long haul, this increases the quality and quantity of your lead flow. It also increases your average customer value as you are weeding out all the less-than-qualified potential customers up front.

Growing a business comes down to selling more customers or making them worth more. This chapter accomplishes both. You get more clients because your marketing becomes more tailored. And, you make your clients worth more by exclusively selling the highest value people. It feels like cheating because it's so obvious. But here's the great part—*no one does it.* Getting this step right will act as a force multiplier on the remaining contents in this book.

Now that we know who we are looking for, is there any other way we can scale our avatar? Short answer—Yes. And we will tackle that on our next adventure.

READ THIS:

At the time of this writing, I've scaled one company from $5M to $42M ARR, one from $2M to $110M, one from $0 to $100M+, and many others from $0 to $10M+. From these experiences, I've learned that scaling occurs in a repeatable pattern.

DO THIS:

If you would like our help scaling your company, you can get a <u>personalized</u> Scaling Roadmap here (for free): <u>acquisition.com/roadmap</u>.

DO THIS IF YOU'RE BIG ENOUGH:

When you click the link above, if your company is big enough, on the thank you page, it'll give you an opportunity to book a call with my team to come out to one of our Scaling Workshops in Las Vegas at our headquarters. It's the most valuable thing I can do for a business. If you've gotten value from my content, come. It's like that but way better and personalized to your current business context. Hope to see you out here!

SECTION A: ATTRACT

How To Get People To Engage, Who Otherwise Wouldn't, Using Free & Discount Promotions

Lost Chapter Author Note**: *I cut the next three chapters from* $100M Money Models *because they were a little too theoretical. Although I love theory, concepts, and frameworks, I don't think a lot of people need them. People just need to know what to do. But if you like understanding the principles I cycle through to create promotions that crush…these next three chapters are for you.*

March 2016.

I stood to the side of the stage. I looked back at the thousands in the crowd. No one knew me. I was 26 at the time. Most were older than me. I checked the clock. I was up soon. My heart thumped so loud I heard it in my ears.

The emcee read his notes to introduce me. I planned to talk about how I pre-sold each of my gyms to full capacity before opening, with no money out of pocket. I repeated my talking points in my head.

Please welcome to the stage Alex Hormoziiiiiii.

My name snapped me into focus. I was up. I stepped on stage. The bright lights shone in my eyes. One thought calmed me, *"At least I only have to talk about something I know."*

I began. My slides were bare. Black and white text with a few images. I felt silly seeing all the other speakers' presentations. They were all so professional. And here I was, a kid in a neon green fitness t-shirt who had been broke only a few years before.

So, I explained the same process I had outlined at the beginning of *$100M Money Models* about our Free 6 Week Challenge. How it worked and the numbers behind it. I told everyone exactly what we did, and how we did it. I'm pretty sure I ended my speech with "So yea, that's it."

When I got off the stage, I exhaled a sigh of relief. As I tried to exit the venue, everyone was leaving too. To my surprise, I got mobbed. The talk transformed me from an unknown kid to someone worth listening to. People surrounded me several rows deep, firing questions.

Do you have a course? Do you have a coaching program? Can you do what you just went over at my gym? My friend has a gym, is there something of yours I can send him?

It was unlike anything I'd ever experienced. It took me 60 minutes to make it from the door of the venue to the men's lavatory 30 feet away. And even there, someone followed me and asked me questions while I was peeing.

My answer remained the same "Nope. I'm only a gym owner. This is what I do. I don't teach it. That's not my business. Sorry."

For the next two days, people asked an unending stream of questions about my presentation. Every time I found myself alone, a new person would dart over, *"got a sec?"* It felt pretty cool. No one had ever paid me that much attention. And as far as I was concerned, I didn't know anyone else liked this stuff. The marketing world was so new to me.

To this day, I still don't know why folks at that conference took so much interest in me. But I was on my own. I had nothing else scheduled. And it was nice to be recognized as "good at this". It was my first sign that there could be more for me.

The event was my first big exposure. It also went hand in hand with what my mentor at the time had suggested I do. *"You should be teaching other people how to do what you do."*

I walked away from the event with a pocket overflowing with business cards and tons of new contacts saved in my phone. 'John M - Guy with beige jacket - supplements' and 'Marcy-owns weight loss clinic - texas'.

Once I got home, I plugged all the names into a spreadsheet. There were over 100!

I had no idea what I was doing, but I knew I could probably help them. So I reached out to them about a week after the event. Many were in adjacent industries like chiropractors or dentists. Some were selling supplements online. Others had online fitness businesses. I didn't know anything about that, at the time. I just knew how to help gyms.

Ironically, the concept of selling a course or program seemed very foreign to me. I had always sold services. But, I had no idea how I would do that here. So I created the first offer for what would later become Gym Launch by <u>giving something away for free</u>: me.

I'll fly out to your gym. I'll spend my own money on marketing, I'll work your leads. I'll close them. Then I get the cash that I collect, and I'll give you the customers for free. I'll show you how to sell supplements. I'll give you my nutrition program. I'll show you how to fulfill them. And I'll show you how to convert them into memberships. Again, for free. I only make what I sell.

Sounds like a Grand Slam Offer? Yep.

I did this for 33 gyms and it took me 18 months of flying around the country to do this model. As you can imagine, it was easy to sell. After all, it was free. It's how I made my first million dollars (outside of my gyms).

And I made it all, starting with a free offer.

Why I Use Free & Discount Promotions

Whenever I get into a new market, I almost always start with something free or massively discounted. I do this for a few reasons. First, I don't know what I'm doing yet, and don't want to sell people something until I'm certain it's exceptional. This gives me wiggle room and forgiveness if it's still a little rough around the edges. Second, I like having testimonials, and the fastest and easiest way to do that is work for free in exchange for testimonials. Third, if I haven't done something before, I tend to lack conviction. So offering it for free or at some massive discount helps me actually close the first few sales (don't be mistaken, I still had to sell people on taking that offer). Fourth, when you start for free, it's also easy to get referrals and start generating demand.

Get Flow. Monetize Flow. Then Add Friction.

Given those reasons, understanding how to promote your Grand Slam Offer is core to getting initial traction and generating your first leads. From there, you can add friction and monetize more aggressively. That being said, if I can continue to build in more Grand Slam Offers to upsell someone over time, I will keep my front end as low as possible to keep my lead flow cranking. This is how I do business. I try to generate demand *first* then I figure out how to make money on it. I feel like too many people try to put the cart before the horse.

In almost every industry I profit from, I begin with a standalone offer, free offer, or a discount offer. They live at the core of my "get new clients" strategy.

So I'll cover each of the three of those in that order. Just remember, free and discount are wrappers *around* the core premium offer we created.

I'm not saying *you* have to do this. I'm saying this is how *I* do it, and it has served me well. If you want to make money fast, ironically, many times it comes fastest from giving things away. Those who give the most, get the most.

<u>Important:</u> The point of creating a promotion is to *enhance* your Grand Slam Offer, not change it. Think of these like wrapping paper. You can wrap a gift in recycled newspaper or you can put it in a Chanel bag with matte black paper and a perfectly tied white bow. What's inside may be the same, but we are making it more inherently attractive. That is the reason for our promotional wrapper. This is especially important when entering cold markets when you must give people a reason to move towards you. It must answer the critical question—*what's in it for me*. We are making it more attractive to a cold audience in order to generate demand flow.

Over the next three chapters we will break down Premium, Free, and Discount offers in more detail.

So—let's learn more about how to make those offers *the right way*.

Premium Promotions

Presenting Your Grand Slam Offer On Its Own

Some things in life are priceless. For everything else, there's Mastercard.
– Famous Advertising Campaign

I walked into the smoothie shop where I worked. My friend sat in the back leafing through a magazine (because magazines were still a thing). I had my lunch in my hand for later, a burger and some waffle fries from next door.

"You wouldn't believe this," he said. "Check this out. This dude bought a burger for $50,000. That's insane."

The burger had gold flakes and exotic caviar on it. But what I remembered thinking at the time was, *"how much money did this guy make to be able to buy a $50,000 burger?"*

"Who bought it?"

"I don't know, some hedge fund manager dude. They said he makes like $50 million dollars a year."

50 million dollars. The idea stunned me for a moment as I tried to wrap my head around the size of that number. That was almost $1 million dollars per week.

When I did the math, I realized if he worked 2,000 hours in a year, he made $25,000/hr. It cost him two hours of his time to afford the burger. Then I did the math on my own income of $6.75/hr. It would cost me the same two hours to afford a burger, fries, and a soda with tax from the place next door—$13.50.

To him, given his income, it wasn't even insane, it was the *same* as me buying a burger.

That's when I realized the power of infinite returns. Basically that there is no cap on the upside, but you can only go down to zero when pricing.

Premium offers work much the same way. While everyone buys traffic on their "$6.75/hr" budget, you buy traffic with your "$25,000/hr" budget. And the best part is, you don't need *nearly* the volume.

Here's what ends up happening in reality. Let's say one business makes $100 per sale ($50 profit) and another business makes $10,000 per sale ($9,500 profit). To make equivalent amounts of profit, business #1 needs to sell 190 people at $50 profit to make $9,500. Business #2 only needs to sell *one*. Here's how it would work in the real world.

If you spoke to those same 190 sales that business #1 closed and offered them all the $10,000 offer instead, you would likely close about 5%.

Here's the basic math:

5% x 190 = 9.5 sales

9.5 sales x $9,500 profit = $90,250

Compared to:

190 sales x $50 profit = $9,500

$90,250/$9,500 = 9.5x as profitable.

As a result, using a high-value offer would make your advertising 9.5x more profitable. So even though the volume is *far* lower, you end up making *far* more, even when normalized. *And* you only have to deal with nine or ten clients instead of 190, which makes life way easier.

That is the power of premium offers, and that is how they can *crush*.

The big caveat is that you need to:

1) Have something very valuable to provide (your Grand Slam Offer)

and

2) Have a selling process that demonstrates that value.

If I Lost Everything And Had To Start Over . . .

If I *needed* to make money, or make a business owner money, I would not start with a premium offer. I would add on a free or discount money model. Over time, as your reputation improves, you can remove those things. But in the beginning, they are essential for most. Earlier in my career, all my offers were free offers.

The offer I ran with after my original free offers was this:

"Apply & Book a call to see if you qualify for our services."

Not. Attractive. At. All.

But, the copy before the offer filtered for the best gym owners that understood it was expensive.

And remember that one of the *biggest* advantages with premium offers is the size of the ticket you can sell.

There's nothing below $0. You can't go lower. But you can go infinitely higher.

If you're new, start with a free or discount offer to get business in the door. Prove results. Then, restructure to a premium offer afterwards.

Note: You can also layer offers together—as we go over at the end of *$100M Money Models*. Premium offers work well as the "second" offer you give after a free offer. But they'll only work if you demonstrated value in the first offer.

Goal of Premium Offers

The goal of premium offers is to sell the client the best outcome available for themselves. You ask the client to buy the thing that will most likely result in them achieving the greatest outcome. That being said, this is not "better" or "worse" than any of the other offer options. It's just different.

For the following "Pros and cons" section, I'm going to flip the script. You're gonna teach me the pros and cons of a premium offer as though we were working together. Thanks for keeping me on my toes!

Pros of Premium Offers

#1 Simplest Math & Fewest Moving Parts

Me: Why would we do this really expensive thing? I doubt many people can afford it?

You: If you're only selling one core "thing," then the math gets pretty simple. You pay $XXXX for YY Leads/Calls/Appts, and you close Z sales @ $VVVV money. That's about it. You just look at what you spent and what you made.

Me: Ah, okay. I get it. Having fewer things to sell makes this easier because I only sell this one expensive thing.

#2 Only "Quality" Customers: Decreases Operational Drag

Me: But we're only going to have a handful of customers compared to a cheaper model?

You: People who come in on premium offers are, in general, the most qualified customers. This decreases the amount of "sifting through the poo" to get the best customers. We "skim" with the marketing, but by doing so you pay a premium for the cream instead of all the milk.

Me: Okay, I get it. So we're *okay* with the fact that we might only sell 10% as much lemonade. Because the lemonade we sell will be more profitable, and our clients will be easier to deal with. That sounds like a good thing.

#3 No Discounts or Incentives: High Lead Quality

Me: So we're not going to give any incentive?

You: Anyone who comes in on this type of offer is expecting to be sold. So there are very transparent intentions on both sides. It comes down to how much they believe we can solve their problem and the perceived value of our solution.

Me: Alright, so I may get fewer leads, but they will be way higher quality. So I should convert a higher percentage of them. Well that sounds good! I don't want to deal with crappy leads all day!

Cons of Premium Offers

#1 Most Expensive Cost Per Lead/Can Take More Time To Break Even

Me: But if these leads are more expensive, how can we afford them?

You: It costs a lot of money to get moving on this. Many don't have the cash to drive volume with these offers. It also takes time to get the sales process down when starting out. And with each opportunity costing us so much more, we have less room for error.

Me: Hmmm…okay, so we need to really know what we're doing here OR have a decent amount of money to burn learning.

#2 Must Be a Good Copywriter and Understand Your Avatar Well

Me: So how much do I need to know in order to sell our $900 per month bundle?

You: When getting into a new market, it can be hard to understand the inner workings of a new avatar. Their deep desires and fears. Their everyday struggles. Here's a two-second example: I wouldn't say "working hard" in your business, I'd say "cleaning the bathrooms yet again." Specificity is what gives copy its edge. Unless you know the real world of your avatar, it can be difficult to get them to bite without a compelling offer and *great* copy. Free and Discount offers give us more margin for error on your copy because the offer can push people on the fence, over the edge.

Me: Okay, so I need to really study these health nuts and high performance folks to know what their real desires and fears are. Okay, so I need to talk in terms of that, not just lemonade. And the more specific I can be, the more it will resonate with them and make them want to buy our more premium offer. They need to understand why it's important not to drink lemonade that isn't sourced from our lemonade orchards with our alkalinity profile. Otherwise, they'll just think we're overpriced Minute Maid. Got it.

#3 Must Be Good at Sales Because This Is a Good Old Fashioned Sale

Me: Since I have no discount or anything, how am I going to get these folks to give us money when they've never tried it?

You: The conversion process end-to-end must be dialed in. The sales process will need to be structured based on the client avatar we're pursuing. But, for now, understand that when we want to lead with premium offers, we should already have a proven process *or* have some cash nested away to get one figured out.

Me: Alright, got it. This is a recurring theme. I need to know what I'm doing.

#4 Least Efficient Way to Capture a Marketplace

Me: But I feel like so many fewer people will buy at this price point, even if we do make a lot of profit?

You: If we are looking for volume, a straight premium offer is going to have to hit a lot of eyeballs before getting a bite. This means we show your ads to more people for a smaller volume of results. A more valuable result, but lower volume nonetheless.

Me: Okay, so we may make good money, we're just not going to be the volume leader in the lemonade category. This is a strategic question of how we want to run the business. I understand.

#5 Must Have an Extremely Compelling Offer of a Result

Me: So I have no discounts or trial offers to give people. How am I going to get them to say yes??

You: To optimize our conversion, we may have a small number of people raise their hands and say they are interested in your offer. As a result, you will need to make sure that you have a truly irresistible offer they are getting for their package. Packed with bonuses, creative guarantees, and premium support to merit the higher cost.

Me: Okay, so all that stuff we did from *$100M Offers* is paying off here. We're going to make our offer so compelling it *still feels like a deal* compared to how much they're getting. Okay, I may have to include some guarantees and give them more bonuses to other things they probably would like as well so this still feels like a steal. Got it.

Conclusion

Premium offers are powerful. They can act as standalone offers that will make you money. You don't really *need* anything else. If you have clients coming in already, using this new structure will allow you to 3–5x your prices without changing your services (seriously). Read *$100M Offers* for more information on how to do this.

But if you're just starting out, or your volume isn't high enough, or your cost of acquisition is higher than you can bear currently, then you will likely want to wrap your premium offer with a free or discount wrapper.

So let's talk about those.

Free Promotions

"If it's free, it's for me!"

Free is the most powerful offer of all time and will never expire. Why? At its base it is "something for nothing" or "value in advance". In fact, researcher Dr. Dan Ariely demonstrated something he called the "penny gap". Basically, he showed that 9x more people would take a free Hershey kiss than one sold for a penny. Imagine getting 9x more people by lowering your discount from one cent to free. That's a big difference. And we're gonna harness it.

Most marketers have experienced this first hand. Getting a page to convert on a $1 offer versus a free offer can be a landslide of a difference. That said, making a free offer is the fastest way to see if anyone wants your thing. Because if your free offer doesn't work, it just shows you that prospects either:

1) Don't want your thing—which means you should change what you are giving away for free (or how you describe it)

2) Don't believe you.

3) Aren't actually seeing it because you are fishing in the wrong pond. This can be a targeting issue. (Ex. = running a single ladies promotion to an audience of married moms).

A famous marketer actually tested #2 to prove the point. Once every few years he would run an offer in the newspaper that said, "For every $100 you give me I will give you $1,000 back, call 444-444-4444." No one ever responded. He did it to illustrate the point of believability. It's an amazing offer. But it was so good, it was unbelievable. That's why whenever you give a crazy free offer away, you will always have to answer the next question: Why? Give a good enough reason, and people will believe you. "Going out of business, all products must go in 30 days" is a very good reason to have "90% off all products". If you just said 90% off all products, you likely wouldn't get the same response. So—as long as it's true—give them a good reason. I go into more depth about this in *$100M Leads, Engage Your Leads Chapter, "c) Fraternity Party Planner (my favorite) - Make Up A Reason."*

Now, let's break down some of the pros and cons of free offers. We're gonna flip the script to keep it interesting. Let's pretend we're starting a lemonade stand together. And you are my mentor. You'll be teaching me, the ever-hungry student, all about Free promotions.

Pros of Free Offers

#1 Highest Lead Volume

Me: So if we want the most leads, we should lead with a free offer?

You. Exactly. If we need volume, nothing works better than free. It gets the most leads per eyeball. And that's always useful, especially in a small marketplace— like a local market. And this should make sense. If we only have X eyeballs in a market, then we want as many people to show interest as possible. Free offers get the most possible people interested in your "thing".

Me: Alright. So, if I want to get the most potential leads, free is the way to go. It gets the best, middle, and worst caliber people—in one shot. Then, I get the opportunity to sell *as many of them as I can.*

#2 Lowest Lead Cost

Me: So not only will we get the most volume, we'll also get the cheapest leads??

You: Yes, just by the same logic. You pay for the same amount of eyeballs, but get a higher percentage of those people raising their hands. Your cost per raised hand is less, making "Free" the source of highest volume and by extension lowest cost.

Me: Sounds like my kind of play. Groovy.

#3 Massive Companies Become Massive & Viral By Learning To Monetize "Free"

Me: But won't this make us not legit?

You: Nope. Some of the biggest companies in the world use Free front ends. They rely on how good their stuff is to get people to keep buying after they try it. Here are just a few examples:

. . . Facebook: "Free to sign up and always will be"

. . . YouTube: "Watch & Create Videos for Free"

. . . Dropbox: "Free X Storage"

. . . Uber: "Free First Ride"

. . . Netflix: "Free 30 Days"

. . . Free Ear Piercings (Claire's)

. . . Free Wax (European Wax Center)

. . . Free Month (Public Storage)

The list could go on.

Me: Okay—so the point is, learning to profit from free offers will lower cost of acquiring a customer (CAC) and create high return on ad spend (ROAS) for our business. Basically, how much it costs us to make money. Got it. Then what's the downside??

Cons of Free Offers

#1 Volume Can Be A Double-Edged Sword

Me: So won't all these leads create some other issues for our business? I don't even know if I could handle calling all these people...

You: For some businesses, free can attract "too many" prospects. So we may need to add friction or make the offer less appealing. We also might not be able to handle the volume operationally. For example, if we have manual processes like you meeting with X people per day, it could be a problem. So we add friction. Friction increases lead quality. The more hoops someone has to go through the higher the quality the lead becomes. So the key with free is learning to find the sweet spot on friction to maximize quality volume. Here are a few examples of friction to increase quality of prospects:

Examples of Friction:

1) **Increased Qualifications**. Ex: "To take advantage of this offer you must be over 25 years old, employed, and a homeowner." If you list out qualifications, it decreases your volume but increases your quality. This is friction you can add to your advertising at all points. You'll want to repeat the same qualifications everywhere. Think: the copy, the creative, the landing pages they see, etc.

2) **Increased Information Requirement & Types of Questions**: Ex: "Please fill out this 20 question application before booking a time to speak with our team." The more required information, the more friction you add. Not only that, but the *type* of information you request increases the friction. For example, "First name" is not as "heavy" of an ask as a cell phone number or an income-related question. Beyond that, the format they use to answer can increase or decrease the friction. For example, multiple-choice creates less friction than open-ended long-form questions.

3) **Increased Number of Steps**: If you make someone take more steps, fewer people will take them. Prospects will drop off at each point. So, you'll get *fewer,* higher

quality people. And you may lose otherwise qualified people. For example: a one-step email opt-in will get more people than a 5-step form. This counts double if they have to certify their age, fill out a form, watch a video, then schedule themselves. That's why finding the "sweet spot" is so important. You want just enough to weed out the weirdos but not so much that you lose some lazy whales.

4) **Forced Consumption**: Forcing a prospect to consume sales material is my favorite way to increase quality. But, it cuts volume. With technology, we can force a prospect to watch a 40-minute video before any call to action appears on the page. By doing this we *only* allow in people who have been pre-indoctrinated. This is a good strategy when you advertise to a large audience and eyeballs are cheap. That said, in other settings the volume is just too low to justify this friction. You can also add it between steps later on once you've *earned* a little more attention from the prospect. This accomplishes the same goal, a different way. Ex: between a first and second meeting. No matter how you do it, forcing consumption cuts volume but increases lead quality.

5) **Advertisement Length**: This is a close cousin of forced consumption but different enough that it's worth outlining. The length of your ads, copy, and videos before they see the call to action increases lead quality. The simple time commitment alone increases friction. Ex: Watching a two-hour video instead of a 30-second video increases friction. You will get fewer clicks, but those clicks will be worth more.

Me: Oh my. What a thorough answer you provided me here. I can think of a whole host of ways of increasing friction to dial in our lead process to get it "just right" for selling our offer.

#2 Some People Have No Intention of Buying.

Me: But won't some people just be here for the free stuff and not want to buy??

You: Yes, this can waste resources if we are giving something away that has an actual cost. Ideally we avoid these scenarios, which is why offer design is so important. But it still always comes down to math:

Free Money Math

If you spend $1,000 on ads

Get 500 Leads

Half are unqualified (250)

And half are qualified (250)

Compared to . . .

$1,000 on ads

Get 200 Leads

80% Qualified (160)

20% Unqualified (40)

Which campaign was better? Our team may feel better about #2, but according to pure dollars and cents, #1 is better. So, make sure to provide value without overextending ourselves. This way, we can use the higher volume and let friction skim the cream off the top. This is how we harness the power of free.

Me: Got it. So—as long as the math makes sense, I'll still probably make more sales, I'll just have to wade through some tire kickers. But, I can create some friction to reduce those guys. And worst case, I make sure my free offer doesn't overextend us but is still valuable enough to get them to want it. Exciting!

Free Brings Broke People Myth

Hopefully you saw some of the pros and cons on free from our little example. Personally, I'm a huge fan of free offers. A friend once joked to me "Everything you sell is free and yet somehow you end up making money!"

Because I am such a fan of free offers, I want to take a moment and pound any limiting beliefs you have about "free" into dust.

When we showed gyms how to use free offers, they'd say... "They're all gonna be freebie seekers and not my ideal customer."

Right and wrong.

We've run four independent split tests of *free* versus *premium* offers. Each test had 10 representative markets.

You know what was the same between both…the gyms' sales closing percentage. As in, if they had 10 "free" offer respondents versus 10 "non-free" offer respondents, the close rate was the same. So being "non-free" offered no advantage in close rates or *average ticket size* over "free".

But you wanna know what wasn't equal between the two? The volume and cost of the leads. Most times going from a non-free to a free front end *decreased* lead costs by five times or more.

Pro Tip: Free Makes More Money

The reason the math is in favor of free is that most times people want to run a premium offer and sell at "free offer" prices. That's where you get messed up. If you know the lead cost is going to be 5–10x higher for a premium offer, your prices should be *at least* 5–10x higher. This may be hard to grasp emotionally, but it's just math.

You need to make what you are selling worth more if you want to play with premium offers. It is the #1 mistake I see when people are comparing them. They are not fair comparisons, the Price, Prospect, Process, Promotion, and Product should ALL reflect a *Free* offer structure or a *Premium* offer structure. You can't just mix and match, they are entirely different acquisition strategies. But, despite this, I have run the tests with the same price point. Free beats premium hands down unless they've truly mastered the art of high-ticket selling.

That being said, I'm not saying free is for every offer, every time. But, I am saying that if you learn how to harness it, there are some ways to layer "free" into a powerful money model.

Bottom line: If I only had one offer to make to convert or my family would be killed, it would be a free offer. I'd rather wade through crappy leads, then figure out how to add friction, than look at an empty calendar.

Now that we've covered "Free," in the next chapter we'll explore the pros and cons of Discount offers.

Discount Promotions

A discount turns wants into haves. Why pay more when you could pay less?

Understanding Discount Offers

Fundamentally, "free" and "discount" offers operate very similarly from a money model perspective. Basically, they create a perceived value discrepancy that on its own can drive action. That being said, I personally am *not* a big believer in "marginal" discounts (say 5 to 25% off). It's just not enough to drive real behavior in my opinion, and basically just cuts into margin.

Instead, we're going to be talking about *massive* discounts (50% or more). Those are the types of numbers that people respond to. And they drive action from a population *that wouldn't otherwise act*. And that's what you have to accomplish with a free or discount offer—*it has to get people who wouldn't otherwise consider it to respond*.

Note: most of the time when talking about discount offers, they will only make up a component of your offering, not the entire thing. While there are a handful of notable exceptions, in most instances a discount offer is a "piece of the thing," not the "entire thing". With hope, that makes sense. If it doesn't, the examples will illustrate it.

Four Ways To Display Discounts

So let's imagine we start a lemonade stand. I say to you, "I want to try one of these discount offers out. What do you think? I think we'll be able to get more people to respond to my efforts with some sort of discount, but I don't know where to start..."

"Great question. You're going to have to test it, but I'll show you the framework that I use to test discounts. It'll automatically get you thinking differently about how to display offers from here on out.

"You see, there are four ways you can display a discount. Knowing them is important. People will respond differently to the same discount displayed differently. There are probably others, but these are the four that I find most common and have been tested and used effectively. Let's look at our own business and try all four. You'll notice that sometimes it 'fits' and other times it doesn't. Whether we are selling something premium or in higher volume, the price of the offer many times informs what will make the most sense for us."

Let's imagine we have an ultimate lemonade bundle that is three bottles a day for $30 per day (the numbers don't matter). Well, that's what we're going to promote four *different* ways.

<u>"New Client Special" First Week of Lemonade $29 Instead of $210</u>

1) Percentage Off

   a) Percentage Off: "New Client Special," 87% off first visit

2) Absolute Amounts Off

   a) Absolute Amount Off: "$181 Off First Week" (Normally $210)

3) Relative Equivalent Off

   a) Relative Equivalent Off: "Save A Steak Dinner," *said in negative (what you save in relative terms)* or

   b) "Less Than Going Out To Lunch," *said in positive (what it costs in relative terms)*

4) Simply the Discounted Price

   a) Simply Discounted Price: $29 New Client Special

Do you see how different these all look and feel? It's the same exact promotion just communicated differently. By cycling through all four, you can test which resonates best in your audience. And if you find multiple winners, even better! It gives you more bullets in the chamber when a promotion fatigues.

Before you just read to the next section, think about other ways you could use a discount for your own offer. Just do the exercise in your head and flex your brain muscles.

Pro Tip: Use Absolute Prices When Talking about Understood Products and Services

In order for a simple discounted price with no other elements around it to be effective, the service will usually have to be one that's well understood. People should already have an idea of what it costs. This is where discounts do well. If you discount something that people don't understand, the offer won't be effective. The only way around this would be to state the price, then state the discount (like in the absolute Amount Off example above). An example that would *not* work with this would be 50% off agency retainer. No one knows what the agency does or how. And agencies have a wide range of costs. So there would likely be a better offer that could be made that would be more easily understood.

Just like before, we're gonna flip roles and have you explain the pros and cons of discounts to me as though we were considering them for our business.

Pros of Discount Offers

Me: But wait, so now I know how to display discount offers. But why would I choose a discount offer over a free offer to get more leads, if free is the most powerful?

You: There are a host of benefits that discounts get that free offers don't provide. You must match the right tool for the job. Let me explain…

#1 Lots of Cheap Leads Within the Law

Me: So it's illegal to market free stuff??

You: Of course not, but in some countries if you have any stipulations or creative offers around "free," they are forbidden. Discounts allow us to advertise compliantly and still generate a decent amount of lead volume. This is especially true when compared to a premium offer, the only other alternative.

Me: Got it, so it allows me to market in ways I otherwise wouldn't and still get good lead volume.

Note: If you are in a heavily regulated industry, state, or country, then a discount offer may be right for your business.

#2 You Actually Collect Some Money

Me: So we collect money for people who buy the discount. But won't that not amount to much?

You: Correct. It won't amount to much money, but it can still help liquidate acquisition costs. But we will never build our business to use this money as the *real* way we are liquidating our costs. This is just the first way for us to attract and transact with a customer.

Me: Got it, so I can collect some cash up front that I wouldn't otherwise, which is nice, but I shouldn't rely on it to fund my marketing efforts.

#3 People Come in Expecting to Spend Some Sort of Money

Me: So I guess the difference between these leads and free leads is that these folks at least expect to pay for something, so it won't be a shock for them.

You: Honestly, this is more of a mental benefit than anything in my opinion. Many business owners/employees have crazy limiting beliefs around selling and consumer-buying behavior. (Not you of course). So giving them something where they feel like the prospects are coming in or opting in ready to spend money makes them more invested in the selling process. Close rates on the initial discount tend to be higher, but still the same on upselling the core offer to the individual, which really becomes the "second" sale.

Me: Got it, so the discount is really for me and my team more than an actual benefit, and we're still going to have to focus on the second sale which is where all the money is really made.

> **Pro Tip**
>
> This is mostly due to the conviction of the salesperson, *not* because people are inherently more willing. A good salesman will sell the same % of free vs non-free leads (assuming the funnels and sales environment are the same). We have tested this four separate times in our business. I've tested it so many times because it still continues to amaze me. But—for whatever reason—it makes people feel better about selling, which is fine. This is especially important when dealing with a small business owner with limiting beliefs. Sometimes you just have to meet them halfway.

#4 The Two-Step Sale (Probably the Biggest Benefit)

Me: So if I'm doing some sort of discount offer, I can collect their card over the phone. And it's an easy sale. But it paves the way for me making future sales more seamless *and* I can charge penalties for other things I may need them to do or adhere to during the sales process.

You: Exactly. If utilizing discount offers for lead generation, they can help eliminate things like "no-shows". This is important when you have a service where the time/cost of the individual is real (like a doctor's time). You want to eliminate no-shows as much as possible. Utilizing a discount offer over a free offer solves this problem for the most part because people will typically show up for things they pay for (at least 85–90% or more). For us, if we want to use this in our lemonade business, we can set a follow-up phone call in 7 days after their discounted period is over to see what they think. We can say that if they don't show up to this appt, we charge them some sort of fee to make sure they show up.

We can use this strategy as a part of a two-step sales process beautifully (which in my opinion is probably the primary reason I would use discounts).

Me: So if I want people to do multiple things before I sell them something more expensive, having a discounted front end makes sure that they do it, and gives me an easy way to create initial trust to lead to future upsells seamlessly. I like it!

#5 Discount Offers Make Upsells Smooth As Buttaaa

Me: So now that I have the person's card on file from the first transaction, I can just ask them, "Do you want to use the card you have on file?" for my next upsell. That's so easy and seamless!

You: Yes, the whole point is we offer something valuable that's *not* our core offer away for an insane discount with the intention of getting leads and getting a card over the phone to get the "thing" at a designated time. The prospect then comes in at that designated time and is upsold something far more expensive after receiving the initial "thing".

An example of a two-step sale would be us giving away a heavy metals test consultation for $19, then upselling the prospect into a $2,100, 10-week lemonade detox plan once we meet with them. So it would look like this:

Ad→ Opt in→ Phone Call for $19 Promo, Set appt→ Shows up for $19 Appt→ Gets Value→ Schedules follow up appt for $2,100 treatment program sale→ Shows up at second appt and is sold.

You would be amazed at how many more people will buy when they don't have to take their card out. It's why Amazon's one-click purchasing, Disney's money wristbands, and so many other institutions attempt to eliminate this friction. They know they will buy more so this is us using that to our advantage.

Me: Got it. And it would help me get around the pesky "I forgot my card at home" obstacles because I would already have the card on file!

Pro Tip: It's Easier To Upsell Than To Sell

Some people call this the "foot in the door" principle. Basically, once you get someone to buy something (even a small item), the likelihood they buy from you again goes way up. Discounts as a front end give you this benefit. It allows you to turn prospects into customers (an important shift). Then, you can *upsell* those customers into your main offer—with the added benefit of a "card on file" close and some built in trust from whatever you delivered with your discount offer.

Author Note: Add Steps As Price And Complexity Increase

The more complex the thing you sell is, or the higher the price, the more time a prospect will need to spend with you in order to buy. You can do this all at once (think weekend seminars) or over time (think multiple sales calls). Both work. If you're having a conversion issue, you may simply be spending too little time with the prospect before asking for the sale.

Pro Tip: Give Away Lower Cost Time If You Can

The other way of solving this problem (my preference) is to *not* give away the doctor's time. And instead operationally fix the first visit so it's something a front desk admin or an assistant can handle. This would be like a prospect coming in for braces, filling out all the required information, taking X-ray pictures, applying for financing (pre-approval), and everything "else" that needs to be done. This allows the business to use the doctor's time only on the most-qualified candidates.

Typically, once the person has come in, you can set the follow up appointment for the "sale". By doing it this way, you eliminate the cost of no-shows while also pre-qualifying all candidates and putting them in the best situation to say yes when they come in the next time. In person, you could also easily close a card for a no-show fee on the next visit. This all but ensures the person will show, ready to buy.

I call this strategy the Proprietary 5 min Appointment Method (feel free to swipe it). If desired, the doc can squeeze the person in between appointments for 5min just to say hello and set up the next in-depth appointment where a treatment plan would be recommended and sold. This would allow them to be able to take appointments all the time instead of during a less than desirable tiny window of time for "new patients". Increasing the available time slots for appointments will improve the percentage of people who schedule more than just about anything else.

Cons of Discount Offers

#1 Giving Away The Farm

Me: But aren't we giving away the farm with this discount offer?

You: Well, it depends what we are discounting. If we always discount our *core* offer, then people will become trained to buy only at discounted times. No bueno. This is why we aren't going to use this as our business model, just a way to acquire customers. The only time where true discounts on our core offer works is if our pricing model is to wildly increase your prices during the "regular season" and live off the discounting. Clothing retailers live this model. But again—it can become a double-edged sword. That's why we're going to "splinter" our offer into tiny pieces and just give a core component at a discount—not the whole farm.

Me: Ah, got it. So we're just giving a sliver away as value to get the card on file so we can upsell more later, not making it our entire business.

#2 Bargain Hoppers

Me: Won't this attract bargain hoppers like the freebie seekers?

You: Again, this comes down to what we are giving away. This was the "issue" with Groupon way back in the day. People started to notice that these customers had no desire to buy the "main thing". But most of the businesses that complained about this did not know how to structure their offers to automatically qualify prospects to *become* customers of their core service. We shouldn't see people as customers if they buy the discount. We should see them as qualified leads.

But we can resolve both of these issues with intelligent offer structure, which I will cover when we hit Advanced Offer Stacking in Section C.

Me: Got it. These are really just opportunities for us to upsell, and if we structure it right, there's nothing unqualified at all about these folks. Heck, I buy discounts sometimes then want more!

Discount Offers Conclusion

In my opinion, discount offers can be used with great effectiveness on the front end or the back end. These can massively increase the take rate on all offers. These are wildly powerful. I cannot overstate this.

In my experience, as a front-end offer, discounts tend to work better with "well understood" services—dentists, chiropractors, gyms, haircuts, etc. People have price ranges they understand so the discounts can be attractive to them to generate inquiries. It must be something that people would value receiving a discount from.

If a customer doesn't know what they are getting, a discount on it doesn't really make much sense because they have nothing to compare it to. So if you're in a well-understood market, or have a service that is well-understood, discount offers can be powerful on the front end.

The other main benefit is that discounts almost entirely eliminate no-shows.

Attract Section Conclusion: Brass Tacks

If you are not getting enough response, you probably need to make your front end more appealing. We need to give people *who otherwise wouldn't respond* a reason to do so. Enhancing your Grand Slam Offer with a free or discount front end is the fastest way to do that. This applies whether you are just figuring out your first acquisition channel or whether you are adding an additional acquisition channel. Always remember—Generate Flow→ Monetize Flow→ Increase Friction. In that order. As I said in the beginning, I almost always start with a free or massively discounted offer so that I have something to benchmark and improve upon.

Fundamentally, to make this process work you must know your business and your product better than your customers do. Why? Because all businesses capitalize on an information advantage. As in, we know more about our customers' problems than they do. We capitalize on this advantage by making them aware of all the other problems they are going to encounter on their journey, then capitalizing on that through upsells. This is how you design a winning acquisition strategy.

SECTION B: THE EXPENSIVE CUSTOMER PROBLEM

If you can spend more than your competition to get a customer,
you will get more customers than them.

Lost Chapter Author Note**: *The next chapters were in the final draft of*
$100M Money Models and I cut them last minute because I thought they were
too conceptual. I wanted to focus the book purely on tactics. But, otherwise, I
love these chapters. They'll help you understand the core problem most businesses
face in acquiring customers and the math to describe the problem.

Pay *extra* attention to this section. You may have to go over it more than once. *That's okay.* Learning isn't about who reads the fastest or takes the best notes. *It's about who does the stuff.* <u>Big money comes from this small section</u>. Keep coming back here until you can do the stuff. It will pay off. I promise.

Customer Financed Acquisition

Customers cost money. If you make that money back faster, you can get customers faster. The faster you make double that amount, the faster you can turn one customer into two more. Two into four. Four into eight, and so on. If customers pay you fast enough, you eliminate cash as the bottleneck to growth.

A dollar today is worth more than a dollar tomorrow. And getting customers to spend *more money faster* is crucial for scaling any bootstrapped business. The only reasonable alternatives are loans and investors. These are great moves when you do them at the right time. But doing it too early will probably bite you in the butt later. For that reason, I prefer Customer Financed Acquisition. In other words, I like to be profitable "day one" and stay profitable—*on my own*—forever. That way if I take out loans or get investors, I do it on *my terms*. Here's how I do it.

Customer Financed Acquisition (CFA) *is when 30 days of GP (gross profit) from a customer is greater than the CAC—the Cost of Acquiring the Customer.* In plain English, it solves your cash flow problems. I express CFA like this:

30 Day Gross Profit > CAC

It costs money to get customers. You wanna make the money you spent to get that customer back as profit in the first thirty days. That way you can use that money again to get *another* customer. *Recycling money is awesome.*

30 Day GP > 2x CAC

But what if we could do one better? What if every customer injects enough cash in the first 30 days to pay for <u>two</u> new customers?

And 2x is my "real life" minimum standard. In practice, I want customers to more than just pay for themselves. I want a *2x or more*. If you do it that way, *you only have to buy your first customer.* Then, that customer pays for every other customer and you can grow the business as fast as it can handle. That's the game of CFA. And that's what I'm going to show you how to do for yourself.

You pull **three levers** to make CFA work…

The Three Levers of CFA

"So you're telling me, we can get paid to make money? Sign me up." – Young me to older me

Lost Chapter Author Note**: *Same thing here. Too many math questions from sample readers. And everyone gets scared with math, so I ended up cutting it. But I love this chapter.*

To Grow A Business

You can either: <u>Get more customers</u> **OR** <u>Make them worth more</u>. To grow our business, we do both.

But there's one more variable I care about—*speed*. In other words, I don't just care *that* a business grows, I care *how fast* it grows. And if we're smart, we can have it all. We get more customers, make them worth more, *and* do it fast. And those three elements create the three levers of CFA:

1) Get More Customers→Lower The Cost of Acquiring Customers (↓CAC)

2) Make Them Worth More→Increase Lifetime Gross Profit (↑LTGP)

3) Do It Fast→Decrease Payback Period (↓PPD)

CFA Lever #1: Get More Customers→Lower The Cost of Acquiring Customers

To get more customers, you need to spend more on advertising <u>or</u> lower how much it <u>C</u>osts to <u>A</u>cquire a <u>C</u>ustomer (**CAC**). And the lower it is, the better. You find it by adding money spent on advertising, sales, and their supporting activities divided by the number of customers you get.

<u>Example</u>: You pay a content producer $10,000 per month. Each month you acquire 10 new customers from the content they make.

CAC = $10,000 costs/10 customers acquired = $1,000

But how much money you can spend to acquire customers depends on how much each customer is worth. The more a customer is worth, the more customers you can get. So…

CFA Lever #2: Make Them Worth More→Increase Lifetime Gross Profit

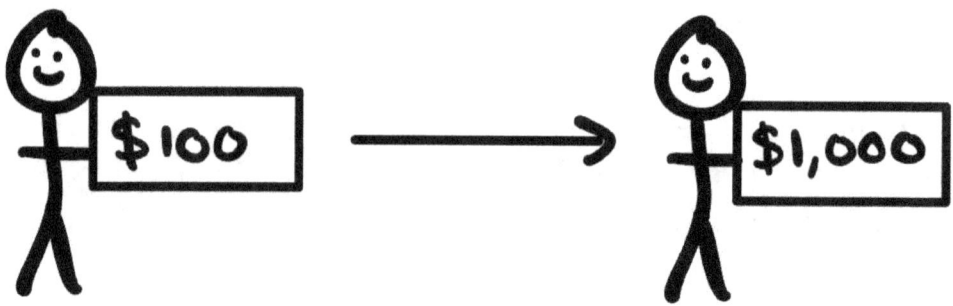

So to get more customers, we spend more money on advertising. But to spend more money on advertising, we need to make more money from the customers we have.

<u>G</u>ross <u>P</u>rofit (GP): This is how much you make from a customer after factoring in the cost of giving them the thing they bought. You find it by subtracting the price customers pay for your thing *minus* the cost of fulfillment. The higher it is, the better.

<u>Product Example</u>: I sell a widget for $100. It costs me $20 to make and ship the widget to the customer.

GP = $100 Price - $20 Costs = $80

<u>Service Example</u>: You sell 10 service packages at $1,000 each. You pay one employee $2,000 to service those 10 packages.

Total GP = $10,000 sold - $2,000 costs = $8,000

GP Per Customer = $8,000/ 10 Customers = $800

If we make more money from each customer, we can spend more to get them. So, we want to make as much money as we can (as fast as we can).

CFA Lever #3: Do It Fast→Decrease Payback Period

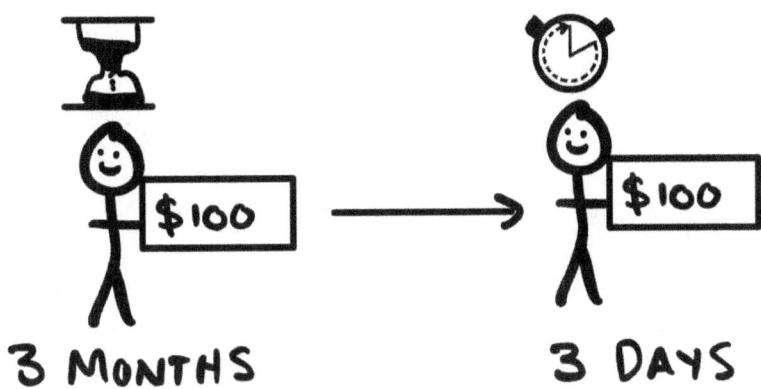

Lowering CAC and raising GP doesn't happen in a vacuum. It happens in time. If a customer pays for themselves today, you can get another one tomorrow. If a customer takes thirty days to pay for themselves, you can get another one in thirty days. Which would you prefer? The first one. Main reason: *you can grow thirty times faster.* In the real world, speed matters. The technical term for this is **Payback Period**. In other words, *how long it takes for your gross profit from a customer to exceed the cost you spent to acquire them.* Math wise, it's when GP>CAC.

Bottom Line: The rest of this section shows you how to make GP as high as possible and CAC as low as possible…as fast as possible (short PPD). The lower your CAC, the faster you break even. The higher your GP, the faster you can break even, get cash flow, and grow. And, we do both—*fast.*

Know The Levers

Lost Chapter Author Note**: Next three chapters are very in-depth math examples. I actually wrote them as part of an internal document that made it into $100M Money Models *then eventually got removed. But, money math is the language of business. This deeper understanding will take you to the next level if you want to go there.*

The three levers of acquisition are: Cost to Acquire a Customer (CAC), Lifetime Gross Profit (LTGP), and Payback Period (PPD). Knowing how to calculate and improve them is how you accomplish Customer Financed Acquisition. We'll dive into each in more depth below. As stated above, this is more advanced so I ended up cutting it. But if you enjoy this stuff…you'll probably make a lot of money.

Cost To Acquire a Customer = CAC

How much does it cost you to make money?

Every business owner always wants new low-cost ways to get new customers. Because the lower your cost to get a customer, the better your ratio is between what you spend and what you make. If you spend $10 to make $1,000 it seems a helluva lot cooler than $900 to make $1,000. This is how crazy wealth gets made.

Here's the problem: most entrepreneurs have never calculated their actual CAC. They report on how much ad spend it costs them to get a customer. Or they think that their content leads are "free". Or, their outbound team they don't consider, only the commissions etc. Then, they're surprised at the end of the month when they're not making any money. That $1,000 sale you *thought* cost you $200 to make, really costs $500. And as small of a difference as that may seem, in some businesses that can be the difference between $1,000,000 per month and $10,000,000 per month. It's *that* important.

So let's talk about how to know it for sure. Unlike LTGP, CAC is a hard science. You can and should know *exactly* what it costs you to get a customer each month, by channel. If you don't, and you were looking for a sign to start tracking…here's your sign. So let's do three examples.

Cost of Acquiring a Customer (CAC): *The cost to get a new customer:* advertising dollars, payroll to a media buyer, creative team, software, sales commissions and salaries, etc.

a) <u>Outreach Example</u>: You use $200 per month email software. You pay someone $3,000 per month to cold email prospects for you. Emails become appointments that turn into eight sales per month. You pay your salesperson $100 per sale.

   What's CAC?

   Total cost for eight sales =

   $3,000 Emailer + $200 Software + $800 Commissions (8 x $100) = $4,000

   Now divide that by the number of new customers =

   Cost to Acquire a Customer (CAC) = $4,000 Cost / 8 New Customers = $500

b) <u>Content Marketing Example</u>: You have two people on your media team that you pay $5,000 per month each. They help you make, edit, and distribute content across all platforms. That content turns into inbound messages and options on your site. Those leads turn into ten new customers. You pay $100 commission per sale. What's CAC?

Total cost for ten new customers =

Media Payroll: ($5,000 x 2) = $10,000

Commissions: 10 Sales x $100 = $1,000

$10,000 + $1,000 = $11,000

Cost to Acquire a Customer (CAC) = $11,000 / 10 customers = $1,100

c) <u>Paid Ads Example</u>: You pay a media buyer $4,000 per month. You spend $20,000 in media (buying ads). You spend $1,000 in commissions per sale. You spend $1,000 in software for tracking and following up with leads that come in. You get ten new customers. What's CAC?

Total cost for ten new customers =

Media Payroll: $4,000

Media Spend: $20,000

Software Costs = $1,000

Commissions: 10 Sales x $1,000 = $10,000

$4,000 + $20,000 + $1,000 + $10,000 = $35,000

Cost to Acquire a Customer (CAC) = $35,000 cost / 10 customers = $3,500

CAC Action Step: calculate your CAC for your business for the past few months. And if you advertise in multiple ways or on multiple platforms, figure out how much it costs you on each. The results may surprise you. <u>Hint</u>: One of the first things we do when we invest in a company is run a full diagnostic on acquisition. Half the time we find a channel or platform that's doing significantly better than others. Guess what we do next…we do more of the one that gets us the best-cost customers.

Now we understand what CAC is, and how to calculate it independent of advertising method. Hooray. Next up, if we can't lower CAC anymore then our next big lever is to increase how much we can pay compared to our competition. Which—we can do by increasing our lifetime gross profit per customer (LGTP)...

Lifetime Gross Profit (LTGP)

The arms race of business.

LTGP: *The amount of <u>gross profit</u> a business collects over the <u>lifespan</u> of a customer.* In other words, how much <u>total</u> money you make from a customer minus everything it costs you to deliver it.

Now, that's easy to understand, but can be hard to figure out if you don't have a customer relationship management (CRM) system or tool that tracks some of these metrics. That's okay though. I'm going to give you some "back of napkin" ways to calculate it.

LTGP Step One: Gross Profit

The first thing you have to figure out is your gross profit. **Gross Profit** is *what's leftover from a purchase after you deliver the goods or service.* Note: this isn't net profit (which is what's left over at the end of the month after you paid *all* expenses). This is just what's leftover on the core thing you sell. You then run your business on this gross profit to pay the rest of your bills (and hopefully have some left over for your pocket at the end of the month).

Author Note: Many entrepreneurs mix up <u>Gross Profit</u> and <u>Net Profit</u>

Gross Profit is money left over after *only* subtracting the costs of making and delivering your product or service.

Net Profit is money left over after subtracting *all costs*.

<u>Product Example</u>: I sell a widget for $100. It costs me $20 to manufacture and ship the widget to the end customer. My gross profit is $100 - $20 = $80.

Also, **Gross Margin** is your gross profit expressed as a percentage of the total price you charge. Gross margin and gross profit get used in a lot of similar situations. Don't let it confuse you. It's the same concept. Gross profit is expressed in an absolute dollar amount while gross margin is the same concept expressed as a percentage. In this example, my gross profit is $80 but my gross margin is 80% ($80/$100 = 80%). That was a good warm-up, let's do one for services.

<u>Service Example #1</u>: I deliver services monthly. I have one account representative per 10 clients. My clients pay $3,000 per month each. My reps cost me $6,000 per month. Let's figure out the gross profit/gross margin.

Clients Per Rep = 10

Revenue Per Client = $3,000

Cost Per Rep = $6,000

So, I make 10 clients/rep x $3,000/mo = $30,000/mo per representative. Assuming I have no other costs for delivering my service, my gross profit is $30,000 Revenue - $6,000 Cost = $24,000. My gross margin is $24,000/$30,000 = 80%. So my gross profit on a single customer is $3,000 x 80% = $2,400. Cool right?

LTGP Step One Action→Figure out your gross profit and gross margin for each thing you sell and your business overall. <u>Hint</u>: you may be surprised that some products you spend a lot of time on don't make you as much profit as you thought.

LTGP Step Two: Figure the average number of transactions a customer makes over their lifetime.

If your CRM tells you this—awesome. But oftentimes, they don't. And even if they do, they're often wrong because data tracking can be a mess (especially if you're starting out). So it's good to understand how to do this money math. I'm gonna give you a few "back of napkin" methods that you use depending on your circumstances.

<u>Disclaimer</u>: Figuring out how many transactions a customer makes on average is always an estimate because everyday customers buy more stuff and the business gets older. As such, lifetime transactions always increase as a business gets older because old customers buy more. So these are the ways I estimate it.

1) Export your lifetime customer data. Sort by number of transactions. Average out that column. Ta-da.

    a) Ex: Avg # of transactions = 4

2) If you have a recurring revenue business, you figure it out differently. This forces us to introduce a new concept—churn. **Churn** is the percentage of customers that leave between time periods. So, if on the first of last month we had 100 customers and this month, of those 100 customers, we lost five, our churn is 5%.

    a) Last Period = 100

b) This period = 95

c) Difference = 100-95= 5

d) Churn = people who left divided by original amount = 5 / 100 = 5%

Note: People get this twisted. Don't be one. If you sign up new clients during this time period, it does **not** affect churn. The same number of original people left. You could sign up zero or 1,000 new clients during the same month. You still lost five of the original one hundred and your churn is still 5%.

LTGP Step Two Action: Figure out # of transactions or churn. Now that we have this figured out, all we have to do is put steps one and two together to get our lifetime gross profit.

LTGP Step Three: If you have a physical products business, multiply average gross profit by # of transactions. Or, if you have a recurring business, divide gross profit by churn percentage.

Physical Products LTGP Example:

Gross profit x average transactions per customer = LTGP

$80 x 4 = $360 LTGP

That's it!

Services LTGP Example:

Gross profit / Churn = LTGP

$2,400 / 5% = $48,000

Bingo. See. Math - no fun. Money math - so fun.

That being said, I want to make an important point. LTGP is the arms race of business. In an auction of attention, *the person that can spend the most to acquire a customer wins* (Dan Kennedy). Or as I prefer to say it—*the business that makes its customer the most valuable, wins*. After all, you can only get CAC to zero, but LTGP can go infinitely high. And in my experience, it's easier to make advertising more efficient than it is to make people stay longer. CAC is about getting customers. LTGP is about keeping customers.

This leads us to the final part of our acquisition trio: Payback Period (PPD).

Payback Period = PPD

How fast do you make your money back?

If you think of what a business is, it's a box where you get a much higher return than the stock market, on far less money. What makes businesses valuable is they are able to get 5x, 10x, 20x returns, in a matter of weeks or months, compared to 10% returns over years.

Payback Period: *the time it takes to break even on what you spent to get a new customer.*

<u>Example</u>: You make $50 per month in gross profit from a new customer. You pay $100 to acquire that customer. You get your first payment day 1, so you get $50 of your original $100 back. Then you get your second payment on day 31, to get the remaining $50 of your $100 back. Therefore, your payback period is 31 days.

I'll be using a hypothetical business (a lemonade stand) throughout this section to illustrate the concepts and frameworks, and to make acquisition models fun and accessible. Most importantly, I'm doing this to illustrate that these models work with *all* businesses including *yours*, whatever it might be.

Let's Start a Lemonade Stand

Alright. Here we are. We've got a fledgling lemonade business. We've got aspirations to become Citrus Kings of a lemon empire. But do we have the skills to do it yet?

Let's say we start with a recurring lemonade model. And let's say for simplicity's sake that we charge $10 per month per customer. And let's say our average customer stays five months, for a total of $50 of lifetime revenue. (Note: add or remove zeroes as desired, this could also be $10,000 per month and $50,000 lifetime revenue, depending on the product, business, or prices you aspire to—the concepts remain the same).

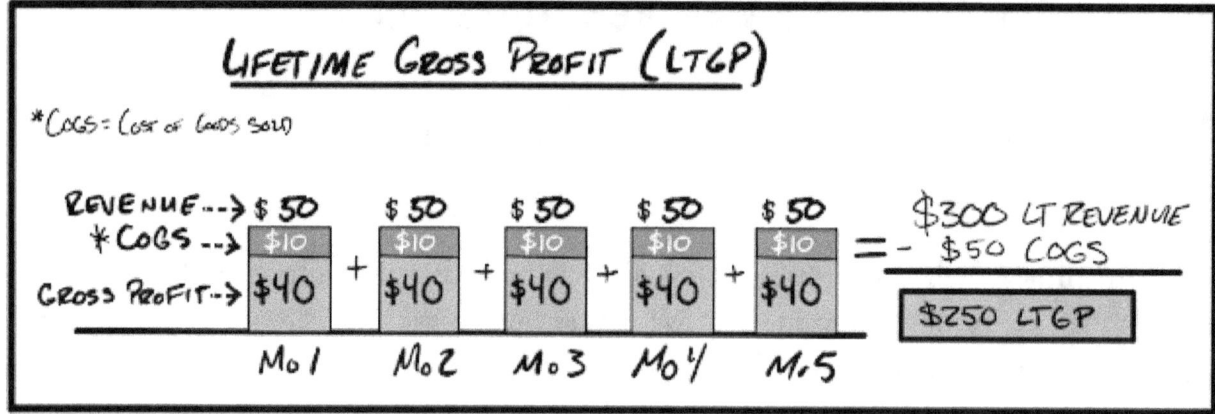

Now let's say we run 80% gross profit margins. In this hypothetical business, we might pay $2 per month to fulfill these $10 per month lemonade shipments for us (delivery costs, lemonade powder, filtered water, etc.). So $10 - $2 = $8 gross profit. That's an 80% gross margin. That means of the $50 we make, $40 of that is gross profit—aka, it goes towards paying our other costs (like paying off the corner neighbor to use their lawn, keeping track of our accounting) and making a profit for us (the owners). In this example, as the average customer buys lemonade for five months, our LTGP is $250. Knowing *only* how much we make (LTGP), it would be impossible to know if our lemonade business is likely to be a rocket ship or a dud. We also need to consider CAC and then PPD to help us fully figure out our growth potential.

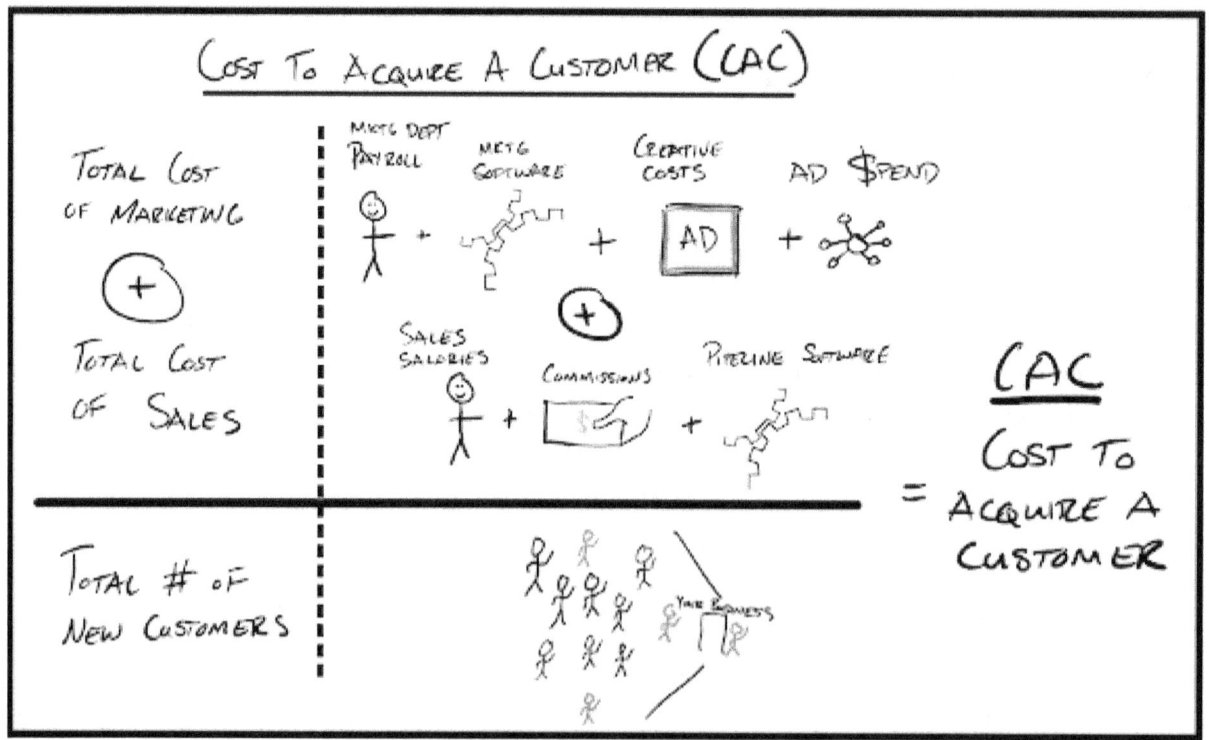

How much is the CAC for a customer that pays us $10 per month? That's the next piece of information we need. This includes *all* the costs that go into acquiring a customer: advertising dollars, payroll to a media buyer, creative team, software that team uses to make advertising, sales commissions and salaries, etc. (If you like pictures, I did my best to illustrate this above).

The back of napkin math way I use to figure this out is by looking back at any time period in the past (last 3, 6, 9, or 12 months):

Equation:

(All Marketing & Sales Team Compensation, Advertising, Software) / CAC
= Total # of Customers Acquired over a Period of Time

Example:

$400,000 Total Costs to Acquire all Customers For 12 Months / $40 CAC
= 10,000 Customers Acquired in the business for 12 months

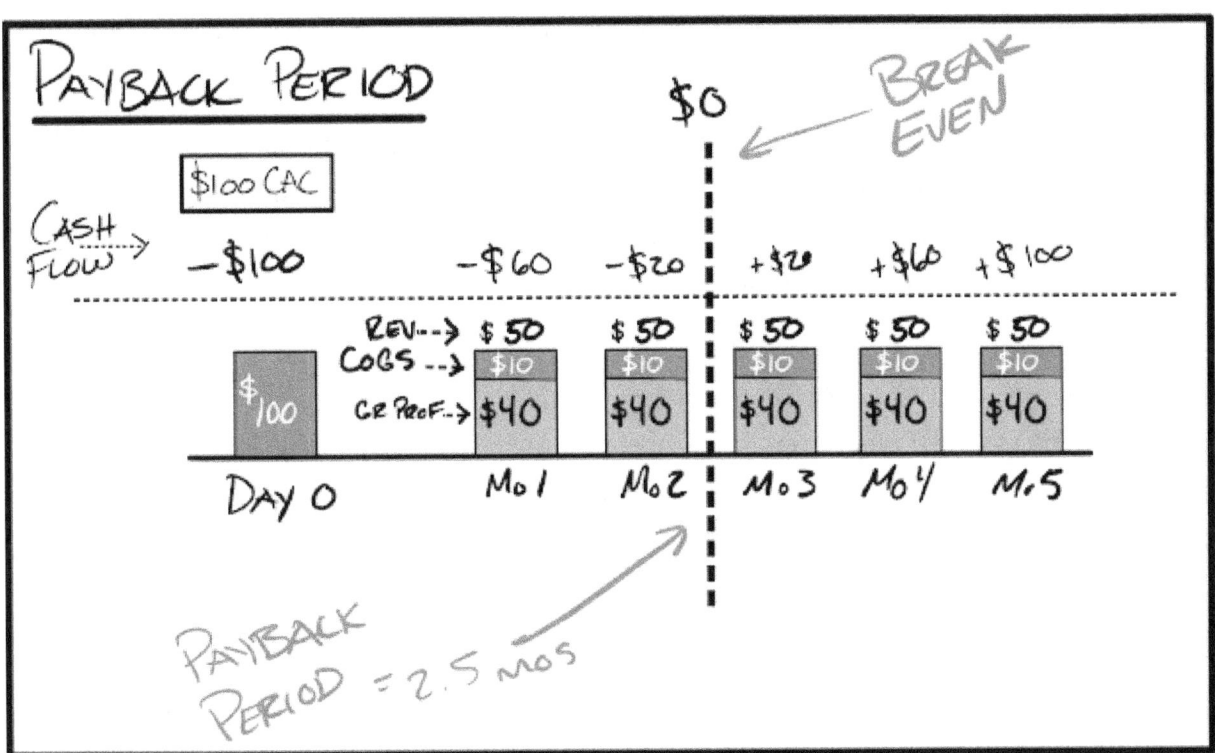

So, how quickly does the lemonade stand pay the CAC back and start making money? Aka - payback period. Payback period is important because it will increase the speed of the cycles in which you can multiply your cash. Doubling our money in one month versus three months may not seem like "that big" of a difference. But it *is*. We're talking about a 4x difference in growth potential. We could double our money in a month (2x), then double our doubled amount in month two (4x), and finally double our quadrupled amount in month three (8x), for a total of 8x our original sum. The three-month example would only double in that same three-month period. So the first business would grow at 4x the speed ((8x/2x = 4x), <u>compounded</u> quarterly. *That* is why the payback period is so important.

Alex's Most Prized Metric: 30 Day Cash (30D Cash)

Getting you to understand Customer Financed Acquisition is literally the objective of this section. What it is. How to achieve it. How to scale it.

A key factor in this process is *time*. If you had unlimited time to pay a debt back, your likelihood of repayment (assuming ethical behavior) approaches 100%. The shorter the window, the less likely. Mastering the timeline of cash flow unlocks truly limitless growth. It got me from $1,036 in my bank account to $100M+ in sales in a few short years...using other people's money to fuel the growth. With that, what is 30 Day Cash?

30D Cash *is the amount of gross profit I can extract from a new customer in their first 30 days*.

The reason 30 days is so critical for small businesses is that 30 days is typically the amount of time *any* business can get interest-free financing—credit cards being a prime example. If I can increase my 30D Cash above my CAC, then it means that I can get free customers using other people's money.

In other words, I max out a credit card with 0 interest to acquire new customers. And by the time my first payment is due (30 days), I pay off the entire balance interest free from the gross profit my new customers have brought me. At the end of the month I now have a 0 debt on my card, which I can max out again next month, new customers (that paid for themselves), and hopefully some profit for myself. This is how you get free customers for life (and get paid doing it).

Let's look at the picture below. I can't play a video in a book, so follow the circled numbers in sequence to understand each of the five points. I'll dive into each below the image.

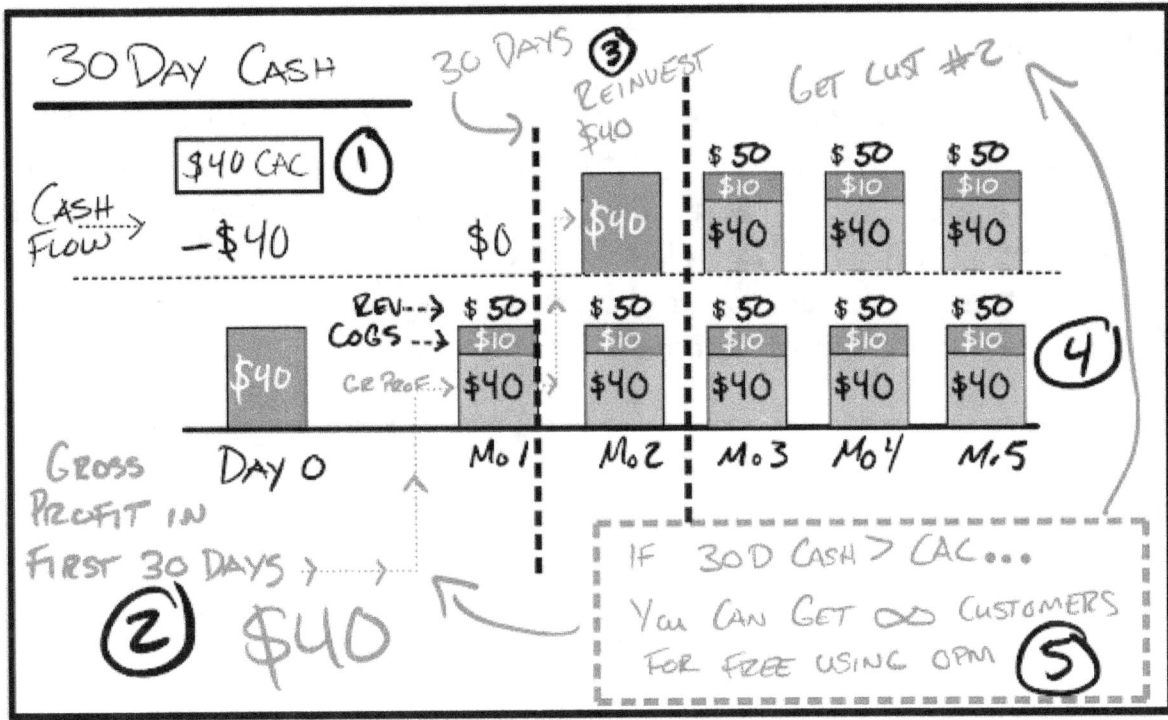

1) Day 0: We borrow $40 from the credit card company to acquire our first customer.

2) Between day 1–30: We make $50 in revenue. Our cost to fulfill is $10. So $40 gross profit remains.

3) Day 30: We repay our original $40 debt with the $40 gross profit so our balance is $0. So after 30 days we have 0 debt *and* a new customer that will continue to spit off more gross profit every month. Then we re-borrow $40 again to acquire another customer.

4) Between day 30–60: We make an additional $40 gross profit from our first customer, which we then pocket for ourselves.

5) Day 60: Our second customer spits off another $40 in gross profit, which we use to repay our debt once more returning our balance to $0. After this is all said and done, we have two customers paying us $80 gross profit per month and zero debt.

Using this process, we can finance each customer using other customers' money (or as some people call it "other people's money"—aka OPM). The only money we need to get started is the first cost of acquisition.

Author Note

This process is intended for businesses to get financing from their clients rather than outside investors. If you apply the concepts, you will have no need for outside capital. There's always a clever way to get your customers to pay for your growth. You just have to look for it. If you already have capital, you can use these strategies to better allocate that money towards your product and your team rather than acquiring customers.

Understanding these three metrics: 1) LTGP (Lifetime Gross Profit), 2) CAC (Cost of Acquiring a Customer), and 3) Payback Period, are the key to understanding how to unlock acquisition. It is the basis upon which we will layer Customer Financed Acquisition: the holy grail of customer acquisition.

Example of the Problem: Normal Lemonade Business

Let's say we learn how to market on a channel (door knocking, email, advertising, cold calling, etc). On this channel, we acquire customers for $20 and our payback period is two months. Customers from this channel will make us $40 in LTGP. Great. Now we have our three variables. Let's look at what running our business day-to-day would look like from a cash flow perspective.

We have no customers. So, we put our pennies together to spend $20 on marketing. After spending that $20, we get *one* customer who pays us $10 per month. It costs us $2 per month to pay an employee to fulfill these products. So we make $8 back from our $20 spent in our first month. In our second month we make another $8 back. And in our third month, we would make $8 again, putting us $4 over our $20 cost of acquiring the customer. Then the customer stays for two more months. We make $8 each month, totaling $20 of gross profit. Hooray—we doubled our $20 investment in five months! Not so fast. Here's how it breaks down visually...

Day 0 (-$20): We spend $20 on marketing.

Day 30 (-$12): We make $10, $8 in gross profit, but it goes towards recouping CAC.

Day 60 (-$4): We make another $10, $8 in gross profit, still going towards CAC.

Day 90 ($4): We make $10, $8 in gross profit. We are finally making money! +$4.

Day 120 ($12): We make $10, $8+ in gross profit.

Day 150 ($20): We make $10, $8+ in gross profit, then the client cancels (sad face).

The business still needs to pay fixed costs like rent, utilities, software expenses, etc. It also needs to, you know, actually pay us as the owners (the point). Based on the above numbers, we're looking at a hard business to grow! But it is very, very common. Notice we don't see our cash returned to us until month three (while still maintaining and running the business!).

Author Note

How much you make (LTGP), how fast you make it (Payback Period), and what it costs to make it (CAC) all factor into your ability to create a wonderful business.

Example of The Solution: Wonderful Lemonade Business

Now let's say you, being the smart entrepreneur you are, come to me and say, "There has to be a better way."

I agree.

Then you go read the *$100M Series*. Then you read it again.

That quickly, you've become a master of acquisition. You figure out a way to acquire customers for less money *and* get paid back faster. Given your newfound skill, let's imagine our cost to acquire a customer is now $1 (CAC = $1) and we're able to pay back that $1 in seven days (payback period = 7 days).

With this new model, we put our money together and spend $1 on marketing with a new channel and method. For purposes of keeping our lives simple, we decided to keep our prices and margins the same. We would make the same $8 gross profit back that first week and $8 per month of profit the next four months, totaling $40.

Here's where it gets wild. Since our CAC is so low and our Payback Period is so fast, we could pay back our original $1 CAC almost immediately. Then we could reuse the $7 gross profit left from the first transaction to go get ourselves *seven more* customers. And from those seven, seven more customers, and so forth. This would be a wonderful business to grow! It's hard to envision with words, so let's break it out visually.

Day 0 (-$1): We spend $1 on marketing.

Day 7 ($7): We acquire a customer who pays $10. We make $8 of gross profit. We cover CAC of $1 and still have $7 left over.

Day 8 ($0): We spend the $7 in gross profit we just made on more marketing. Now we're back to $0 (but that's okay!).

Day 14 ($56): We acquire seven *more* customers at $1 each. Each pays $10 for a total of $70. We make $8 in gross profit each, so 7 x $8 = +$56. Woohoo!

Day 15 ($49): We now have enough money to get ourselves 49 new customers. But we decide we can't possibly handle that many more customers. So we just stick with acquiring another seven. So we spend $7 on marketing in the hopes of getting seven more customers. $56 - $7 = $49.

Day 22 ($105): Success! We get seven more customers from our $7 of marketing, which makes us another 7 x $8 gross profit, and another $56 in gross profit. This is starting to get crazy!

Day 30 ($105): We take a breather.

Day 37 ($113): We keep breathing but realize that first customer renewal comes up and makes us another $8 of gross profit. We didn't have to spend anything for this. Sweet!

Day 44 ($169): The next seven customers renew with $8 of gross profit each +$56. Holy cow.

Day 51 ($225): A week later the next seven renew and generate yet another +$56. Man, printing money is fun!

Day 60 . . . we decide to write a book on acquisition (joking).

The example above is gross profit, not revenue. So this is money in the bank after paying all the cost of fulfilling the customer *and* the cost of acquisition. The only place this money goes is to pay fixed costs (rent, software, etc) and to pay us (the point!). Or the money could go to grow our team, so this month we can handle 14 clients per week instead of seven. This is how businesses grow *without taking outside capital.*

So, how much money did we actually spend in marketing during our wonderful lemonade scenario?

Drum roll . . .

Answer: $1.

Wait, what? Yep. We only took that first $1 out of pocket and spent it on advertising. The rest of the time, we are playing with the "found" money. It's like gambling at the casino with $1, making $8, paying yourself back the original $1 bet, then playing the rest of the time with the $7 winnings. Another way of saying it is: we crowdfunded the growth of our business using our customers and a clever acquisition system.

I've been playing with the house's money for almost a decade now, and by the end of this book, you can too.

Levels of Customer Financed Acquisition

New levels, new devils.

By connecting GP and speed with CAC, I see three levels of CFA.

<u>CFA Level 1</u>: *You make less profit (GP) from a customer than it costs you to get one (CAC) in the first thirty days.* You eventually come out ahead, it just takes longer. This means floating your businesses on life savings, loans, and lines of credit. A big risk. And speaking from lots of experience… it sucks.

And yes, you can absolutely make money this way over the long term. And many big businesses make *all* their money this way. But you have to *already have lots of money* to do it. And most young bootstrapped businesses don't. So I avoid this when starting out.

<u>CFA Level 2</u>: *You make the same profit from a customer as it costs you to get one in the first thirty days.* I specify 30 days because any business can get interest-free money for 30 days in the form of a credit card. If you clear your balance before the end of the month, it works just like normal money. So you can use credit to get a customer, pay it back, and then use it again to get the next customer.

At level 2, since you pay off the card each month, your credit limit becomes your advertising budget. This means it caps how many customers you can get. So if you have a $5,000 limit, you can only get the number of customers $5,000 will get. Of course, you can expand your budget by paying your balance off early, asking for a higher limit, or getting another card. Easy peasy.

The contents from the rest of this section will boost your GP and get you to level 3.

<u>CFA Level 3</u>: *You make more than double the profit from a customer than it costs you to get one in the first thirty days.* This holds a special place in my heart. It's how I've scaled all my businesses. In principle, it means you can double your business every month (or faster). Think about it this way: You pay the balance of your original spend. Then, between the credit and extra cash, you can get *two* more customers. And if you only use the extra cash, you can ditch credit altogether when the GP rolls in.

From that point on——*all customers pay for themselves.* And you can use your extra cash for whatever you want…including getting even more customers. CFA removes "cash" from your list of problems in life.

<u>As a reminder</u>: Making twice what it costs me to get a customer in profit is my *minimum*. My first year of Gym Launch we got $100 back in profit for every $1 we spent. Yes. 100x. Spending $100,000 to make $10M in returns. We obviously scaled as much as we could from that. But then operations limited us...not getting customers. And *that's the goal here.*

If you wonder: *why bother getting more customers when I could just pay myself?* I say, why do one, when you could do both? Once customers start paying for themselves, I can grow my business *and* pay myself. Best part is, when you do it this way, your business grows every month *and so does your paycheck.*

CFA: Playing It Out

You must pass CFA level one to stay in business for the long haul. With a decent product and a good offer, you can bootstrap your growth to level two. Then, you master Money Models—see *$100M Money Models*—to unlock *profitable* hyperscaling at level three. And once you hit level three, cash to get customers no longer constrains your business.

To show you how powerful this is, let's play out CFA Level 3 for your new business. And let's assume you put all extra profits into getting more customers. Over the next 12 months, you would go from one lonely customer to... *an army of 4,095 customers.* Best of all, you'd only have to pay for *the first customer.* The rest of the growth—*your customers pay for.* That's why it's called Customer Financed Acquisition. They finance the acquisition of your new customers! The table below lays it all out.

Months at CFA Level 3	New Customers Acquired	Total Customers Acquired
1	1	1
2	2	3
3	4	7
4	8	15
5	16	31
6	32	63
7	64	127
8	128	256
9	256	511
10	512	1023
11	1024	2047
12	2048	4095

And that's only with a GP at twice CAC! It can go *much* higher. And yes, something else will eventually bottleneck your growth. *And that's OK.* That's life. *But you never want that bottleneck to be cash for getting customers.*

And that's really what CFA is all about. Removing cash, and by extension "customer-getting" as your limit for growth. If I can do that for you, and help you achieve your vision, we've won.

Solution Explained

When you do this right, you don't need to *have* a lot of money to *make* a lot of money. The clients themselves are like pre-loaded bags of money who pay for themselves *and the next customer.*

This is how we achieve forced viral growth. This is how my software company went from $60,000 per month in revenue to $1.7M per month in revenue in six months. It's how my consulting business went from $215,000 per month to $1.8M per month in eight months. And it's how my e-commerce business went from $80,000 per month to $1.5M per month in six months. This. Stuff. Works.

Now from this example you could very quickly see that the bottleneck would *not* be the ability to acquire customers, but to *service* them. I'm not going to get into how to scale a company in this book. The objective of this book is to get you to the point where *scaling*, rather than *acquiring customers,* becomes your problem. It may seem crazy to you, but this is how you become unbeatable. So change your beliefs, and you'll change your business and your life.

The "Normal Business" example is what most businesses deal with on a regular basis. This is why the median small business owner makes $72,489 per year (Source: *Payscale*). There's nothing wrong with that, but given the massive personal risk and investment we take on as business owners, it would probably be easier to drive Uber and make $70,000 per year with no risk, no investment, and complete schedule flexibility. We business owners take the risks and work our asses off because we believe in the *promise of more*, and that's why I'm hoping you're reading this book: the promise of more.

Acquisition masters, in stark contrast, print money. It's the type of business and acquisition process we want to build. And the beautiful part about building an acquisition model like this is that *anyone* can do it *with skill.*

At the end of the day, I believe that having a great business is a choice. Many do not *believe* they can have a great business. They expect 2:1 returns on advertising to be "good enough," when, in truth, with just a few tweaks they could never spend another dollar on advertising again and let their customers pay for the growth of their business. That's what we're here to accomplish.

SECTION C:
ADVANCED OFFER STACKING

"In your heart, you know… that the juice is worth the squeeze."
– Matthew Kidman, The Girl Next Door

Lost Chapter Author Note**: *This next section starts off with a different way of visualizing maximizing lifetime gross profit per customer. I find it to be a more mathematical way of figuring out what to sell and when. After this primer, the remainder of the chapters are a hodgepodge of attraction offers, upsell offers, and continuity offers that didn't make it into $100M Money Models. They were typically either too hard, or too niched. In either case, I didn't think they applied to a wide enough array of businesses. That being said, for the <u>right businesses</u>, they might <u>change everything</u> for you. Think of these as more bullets to add to your potential $100M Money Model. Feel free to skip around the chapters and read the descriptions to find the ones that might work for you.*

In this section of the book, we'll look at what I believe to be the best piece of my winning strategy. Understanding and executing this concept of stacking offers has made me generational wealth. Ironically, I don't think it's difficult. I just think most people don't know the concept even exists. I promised you at the beginning of the book that the deeper into the book you got, the juicier the nuggets would be.

This is exactly what I was talking about. The earlier materials are no less important. They're just foundational. Just as we need to learn how to draw before we can paint. A basic skill begets a more advanced and valuable skill. Understanding offer stacking will allow you to compete in any marketplace, on any traffic platform. It can even be used to starve your competitors. I try to be a good-hearted individual, but I play to win, as should you. The next few chapters are your new winning strategy.

Basic Outline of the Section

The back end informs the front end. That means the more money you make per customer, the more you can spend to acquire customers. Making a Grand Slam Offer is both about lowering the cost of acquisition *and* making more per customer. In this section,

I will show you how to layer or "stack" Grand Slam Offers on top of one another to create higher lifetime value, aka "the back end". So this is making a series of Grand Slam Offers in a row in order to increase how much a client is worth to the business. This is where things get wild.

Back End: The Value Grid

*The business owner who makes his customer more valuable to
his business, than to that of his competition, wins.*
*- (My rephrasing of Dan Kennedy's quote, "He who can
spend the most to acquire a customer wins")*

Lost Chapter Author Note**: *This chapter felt too conceptual. I like it a lot. It's how I
actually think about increasing LTV—which is so important for getting customers. But, alas,
I didn't think people <u>needed</u> to understand it, so I cut it from the* $100M Offers *book.*

Winter 2019.

"Wait, so you sell twice as many people as I do every month, but you make 56x more profit than me?"

"Yeah, it seems like it."

"Holy cow. So I just need to focus on making more per customer. I don't need to get more clients at all."

"Correct."

This exchange happened on a $50,000 consulting day that I had with someone in my space.

They were on pace for about $3M/year in their business. It was profitable, and they were making money. But they were having trouble scaling. When they came out to my office, they expected the conversation was going to be about marketing and sales. But after quickly reviewing their numbers, I saw they were doing fine on that front. The issue was…they just didn't make enough per customer. They had one offer that wasn't irresistible, and had no upsell or continuity. So it cost them about 50% more to acquire customers than it cost me. On top of that, I made 10 times more than they did on that same customer. Literally. And how we did it is the process I am going to share with you right now.

LTGP is the arms race of business. The higher you can make that number, the more untouchable you become. The higher that number is, the more damage you can inflict on your competition. You can eventually starve them out of the marketplace. This is why becoming a world-class marketer is so important. You can make a product as good as you want, but if you can't outspend your competition, your competition will steal your product *and* your potential customers.

Let me give you an example. If you can pay 10x more to acquire a customer than your competition can, you can decide to increase your spending budget such that you compete against yourself until you raise the bar so that no one can buy ads in your niche.

What this means: if you can claim the throne, you can make yourself virtually unbeatable. You can suck up the entire marketplace and make it very difficult for new people to enter. This is similar to a monopoly, except it's legal.

It's the opposite of predatory pricing (where people lower their prices to force people to operate unprofitably) as well. We're actually taking the opposite strategy of providing more value and raising our prices to make so much money that we can afford to be less efficient. As you do this, you continue to increase your market share, increase how much you make, and add more upsells to increase your lifetime value. When someone new comes in, they would either need to have capital to burn trying to catch up with you, or an entirely new way to monetize their customers to beat you.

I'm not going to get into the many, many, many ways to increase lifetime value. That will be the subject of a future book that I haven't written yet. What I am going to do is simply focus on one of the simplest ways to multiply your lifetime value—"stacking" offers.

Many people think of increasing a customer's lifetime value in *sequence* or *stair steps*. A customer comes in at the bottom or halfway, then ascends up. I think this is a very good way of getting people to think about their business in terms of how to increase the value you provide.

Although it's a useful visual aid, a sequence or stair step fails to take into account a key point…not all customers follow it. So, I think of it more as a grid. For two primary reasons: first, with a stair step, the visual depiction makes your brain think that all customers must buy the first in order to buy the second. It depicts the relationship as linear. This has not been my experience. I think the stair-step visual model falls short in that regard (all models have limits) but is a great place to start to get ideas down. But once you have metrics, the grid becomes an invaluable tool. Here's why…

Many times people buy offer #1 then skip to offer #4. Or they skip offers #1 and #2 and buy offers #3 and #5. Or something like that. They don't buy linearly; they buy the ones they *want* to buy or that solve their needs. The value ladder is based on a fractal concept of customers. At each level only a small percentage of them will take the offer with the big jump in price. But it doesn't take into account multiple offers at the same price point solving different needs. The grid is a different way of depicting the same concept.

The second reason I like the grid is that it makes the numbers visual. You can actually visualize all your prospects. And when you add up all the revenue from all the clients in the grid, and divide it by how many people came in, you know your lifetime value. This makes it a nice tactical tool for understanding your CAC and 30D cash value. Both are very important and interlinked metrics for acquiring customers.

A simple value grid is shown below.

TRIAL	CONV TO EFT	TOTAL
⊗		
⊗		
✓ $0	⊗	
✓ $0	⊗	
✓ $0	⊗	
✓ $0	⊗	
✓ $0	⊗	
✓ $0	✓ $200	$200
✓ $0	✓ $200	$200
✓ $0	✓ $200	$200
TOTAL		$600
AVG /SHOW		$600/10 = $60
30D LTV		$600/8 = $75

From this grid, you can see at the bottom, that from 10 prospects coming into the business, eight of them take a simple trial offer, and three of them convert on the back end to a paid offer. This means that the business generates a total of $600 from 10 prospects. They can afford $60 per show. And the amount of money they collect per trial in the first 30 days is $75. This makes $75 the 30D Cash/ 30D LTV.

From these numbers, if I had a credit card, I could put $600 on my credit card to buy ads to get 50 leads, and get 10 of them to walk in the door. This would mean that I could break even at $12 per lead.

But what I'm not taking into account are the very real costs of working the leads and selling them into a trial, which indeed also costs money. Realistically, it would cost probably $600–$1,000 in labor to work the leads and sell them. I'll use $600 for the sake of illustration. That would mean that I would now only be able to pay $0/lead, because all $600 of the revenue generated was eaten up by fixed costs. This is a situation that is all too familiar to small business owners. *It costs too much money to acquire customers.* The reality is it never costs "too much" or "too little". It just costs what it costs. It's up to us to design our business in such a way that we "make more money" from the same customers to be able to not only "afford" them but profit from them.

Here's how. Let's compare these numbers to the same hypothetical business that has gone through this process of stacking offers (what I'm about to show you).

	Day 0	Day 2	Day 2	Day 14-21	Day 30		
	SERVICE	FOOD x4 wks	SUPPS	12MO	PIF	SUPPS 2ND 2	
(X)							$0
(X) CC+NSS							$0
(X) CC+NSS			$200 (85)				$85
(X) CC+NSS			$200 (85)				$85
(X) CC+NSS		$165 (16.5)	$200 (85)				$149
$2500 (✓)		$165x4 (16.5)	$200 (85)			$200 (85	$2798
$1200 (✓)		$165x4 (16.5)	$200 (85)				$1349
$600 (✓)		$165x4 (16.5)	$200 (85)	12 MO	$2000	$200 (85)	$2834
$600 (✓)			$200 (85)	12 MO	$200 (1ST MO)		$885
$600 (✓)							$600
TOTAL $					$8818		
AVG/SHOW				$8818/10 = $881			
30D LTV				$8818/5 = $1763			

"No"

"Yes"

From this grid, we see the business made a different front-end offer. They made a high-ticket offer of some kind with some downsells, then took the person through a series of upsell offers over the first 30 days of their time in the business. Not every person took every offer, but some people did. And those percentages of people add up. All the way to the right you can see the revenue per client. And at the bottom you can see the totals and averages.

Look at the difference in those numbers between the top example (30D Cash = $75) and the bottom example (30D Cash = $1,763). Both of these grids are for the same type of business. *This is the difference between making a killing and getting killed.* This is how you can outspend anyone on any platform.

You may be wondering how some of the people who came in and said "no" to the initial offer still generated revenue. Easy: we offered them a complementary wellness/lifestyle review just for coming in. At this review, we sold them supplements even though they did not want to buy services from us, thereby making money from people who said "no". That's an offer I call "Free With Alternate Revenue Stream". I break it down in depth a few chapters from here.

Pretty cool when stuff actually works, right?

The difference in revenue generated between the two examples is about 14–15x. This is exactly what was happening with this consulting client in his business compared to my business. In the real world, it means that if your competitor can pay only $100 per lead, you could pay $1,500 per lead and remain just as profitable. Utilizing an upsell framework like this can be one of, if not the greatest, competitive advantages of all time. It also gives you enormous "margin for error" on your marketing and allows you the luxury of not needing the "best" marketing of all time. With a series of Grand Slam Offers increasing your lifetime value, you can still crush your competition even with mediocre marketing. Having this type of revenue per lead unlocks scale unlike you've ever experienced. It is the key for unending growth.

So…now that we covered how amazing of an impact this strategy can have on your business, the question remains—how do we do it?

Advanced Offer Stacking: How To

"The amount of money you make is directly proportional to the amount of goodwill you have multiplied by the amount of offers you make." - Frank Kern, timeless copywriter & marketer

Before we dive into this, there is one strong warning I must make. Adding more offers and services is a fast track to adding operational complexity. That makes business *hard*. If you're looking at your own business, you want to look at things that you can do to add revenue that add little to no cost (time, money, or complexity). If something is going to add complexity, it had better be worth it (lots of profit or very little cost)—keep that ratio high.

I think of a conversion process like an accommodating resistance exercise. What it means is that in exercise physiology, the "perfect" rep is a repetition of an exercise that maximally matches your ability to generate force at every point in an exercise, and with each repetition should get proportionally lighter so that you are always at 100% effort at all times. This allows you to work a muscle more efficiently, gaining strength and muscle faster. For example, you're much stronger at the top of a squat than you are at the bottom. This is why experienced lifters add bands and chains to their barbells, it gets harder at the top where they are strongest, and lessens at the bottom where they are weaker. To date, there is no machine/apparatus that does this perfectly. But understanding the concept is how I think about selling. I want to match my ticket price and value perfectly to the buying ability and desire of each customer *without* increasing the complexity of my business. This is where the creative fun begins.

Identify Adjacent Customer Needs/Opportunities

First, I look at all the revenue streams a customer is buying that are related to the core desires I am solving... *power, money, beauty, weight loss, etc.*

Then see if I can create affiliate relationships (a relationship where another business owner pays you to send them customers). *Or* if I can add it in with little to no operations, I'll do that. Adding in a sales consult to sell physical products is an example where the only added complexity is a meeting with the customer. That is usually worth the cost of making lots more money per customer. Here's what the "need" streams look like before and after they have been turned into revenue opportunities:

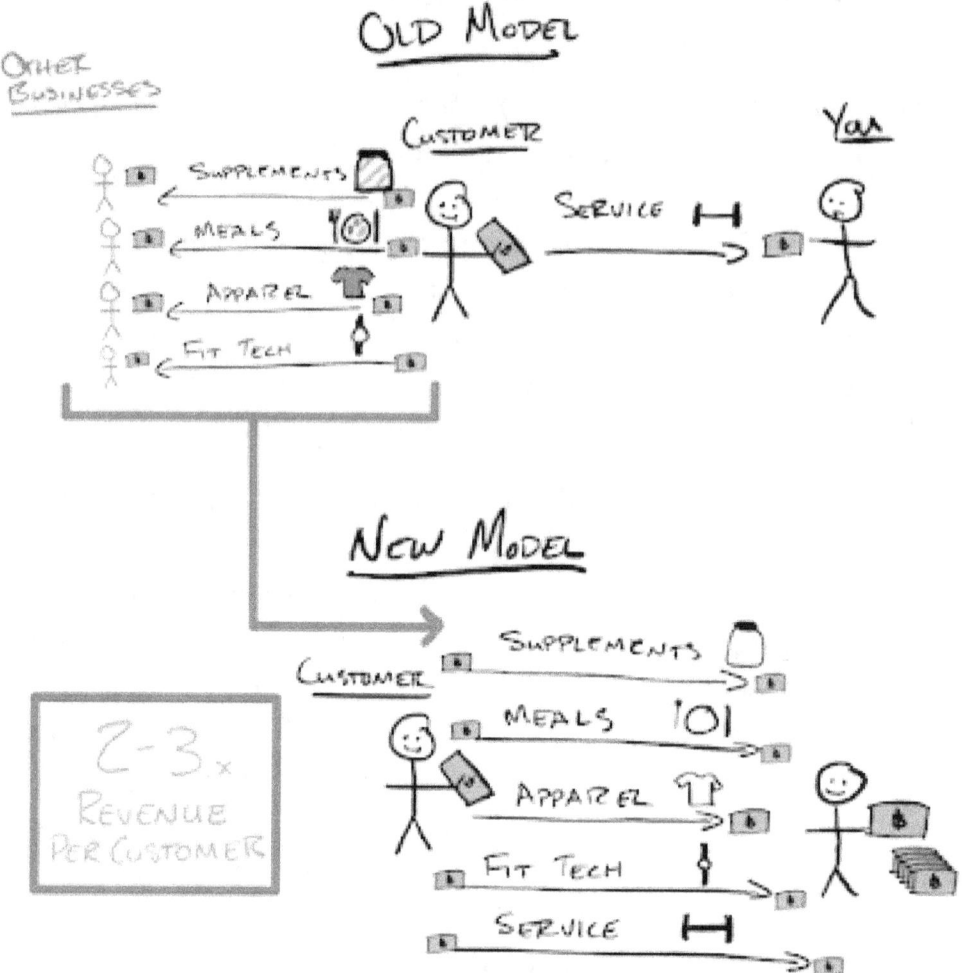

Most businesses refer out lots of revenue. They make recommendations of products or services that are complementary to their own. Over time, though, you'll find that constantly thinking with this mindset adds up. At the time of this writing, I have directly made more than $3,000,000 just in affiliate commissions. Those pennies, since they are pure profit, go straight to your bottom line and should not be underestimated.

For example, take a small business owner who makes $35,280 per year take-home off of $282,240/year in revenue. Adding in $2,000/mo in retail sales commissions may not seem like a lot when compared to the $23,520 their business is making off selling services, *but* the added $2,000/mo takes their take-home income from $35,280 to $59,280, which is life-changing for many. Do not underestimate it.

That being said, if something you refer out makes even more money, sometimes it's worth buying/incorporating that business altogether.

Pro Tip: Free Onboarding

I was able to pay for my entire onboarding team and customer support team by adding an additional call to our onboarding process for new clients. They appreciated the extra support, and I was able to guarantee each of my customers clicked each of my affiliate links when signing up for the solutions they needed. I only had to cover the cost of the additional role in the company for the first month out of pocket. After that, the affiliate commissions I received literally paid for the team. These little "tricks" are the things that add up to making your business unbeatable *while* providing unmatched service to your customers.

Ultimate Offer Stacking Process

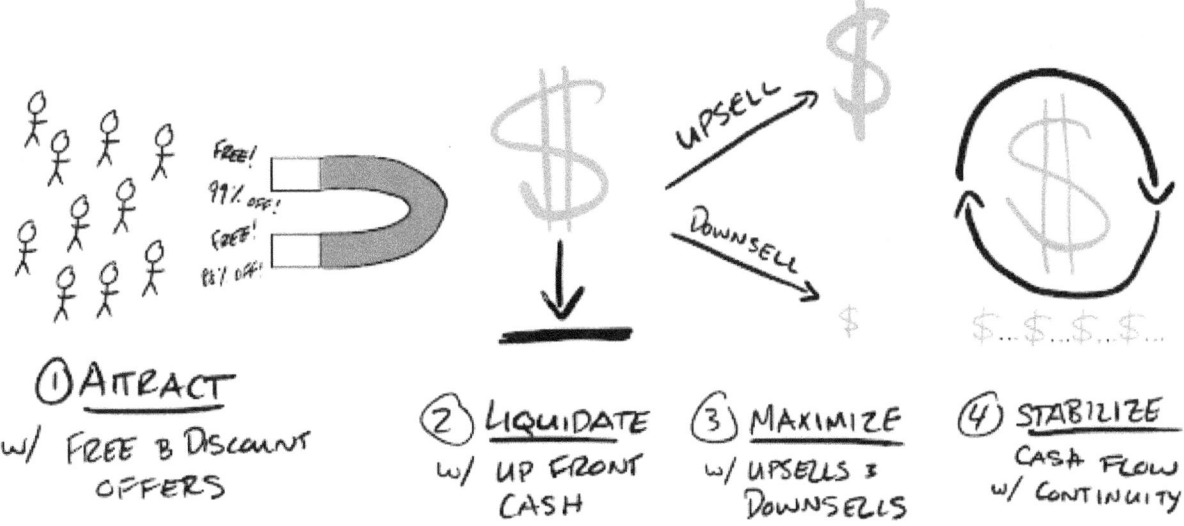

Now, back to stacking the offers. First, we figure out all the needs we can monetize. Next, we decide how we are going to choreograph the sales process. I use this framework for almost every business I work with to weave one of each core offer types together (after obviously using a free or discount hook).

1) Attract → 2) Up Front Cash → 3) Upsell/Downsell → 4) Continuity

This gives me the best of all worlds. The Up Front Money Model allows me to profitably acquire customers. My upsells and downsells allow me to squeeze the most juice per prospect by getting the "whales" to buy big and the "minnows" into my world to buy something big later. Then, finally, I create consistent cash flow by tying in continuity.

Which Up Front Money Model, which upsell, and which type of continuity will rely heavily on the type of business I am working with and how their typical customer-buying journey is structured.

Mind you, after I have done this three-step process, I'll often repeat it again and again. After this person has taken a continuity offer, I may offer additional services (additional continuity offer), then make an offer for them to prepay it for a bonus + a discount (up front cash). So if you were looking at this example it would look like this:

1) Attract → 2) Up Front Cash → 3) Upsell/Downsell→ 4) Continuity→ 5) Continuity #2→ 6) Up front Cash #2

This is how you continue to keep stacking profits in your business. You make money or break even in the acquisition, and you can continue to make offers to your clients. Each time, you're increasing the LTV of the customer, and ultimately, how much you can spend to acquire them.

This concept is *very simple* but *incredibly powerful*. In many ways, I wrote all of *$100M Money Models* to get to this part. Let's do a few examples to really drive it home and make it real.

Sample Weight Loss Offer Flow

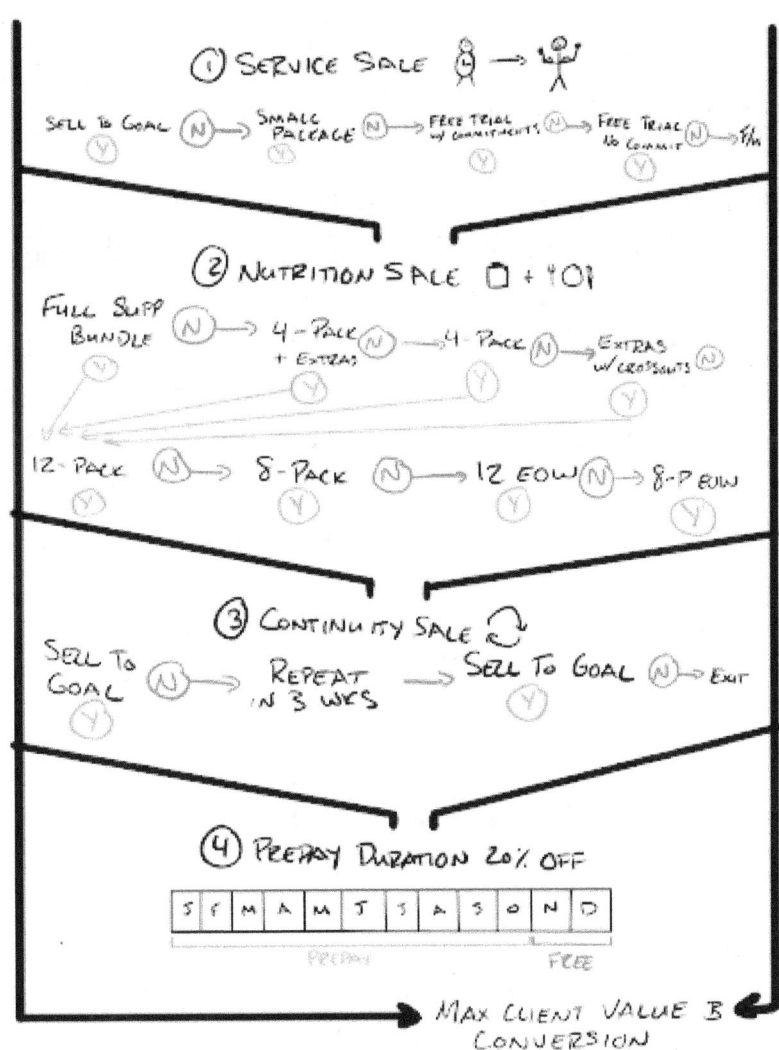

1) Attraction 2) Upsell/Downsell 3) Continuity 4) Attraction

I know this looks complicated. It's not. Each of the sales flows naturally to the next over the span of their time with us. They do not need to take every offer, but we are still going to try. Not only that, in this example, you can see how I am showing the downsells at each step. If you are selling in-person or over the phone, in any one-on-one setting really, these are things that you can do effortlessly. Selling off a page digitally, you will not have this luxury, which is why I am such a big fan of one-on-one sales. It affords you flexibility and allows you to perfectly match the buying power of the prospect with your ability to sell and solve their needs on their budget. And when you do this, and you are competing against people who do not sell like this, you will almost always be able to outspend them.

In the example above, we are selling services, then products. Then we are selling them continuity. Then we are selling them some sort of prepayment discount. Some of these sales can happen in the same conversation. Others need to be spaced out. This is what is actually *happening* to create those sales from the grid I showed earlier.

Sale #1: Service Sale (Up Front Cash)

On a micro-level, we are offering a high-ticket solution first. A certain percentage of customers will take that big ticket offer. But if they say no, totally fine. We transition to a half down version of the same offer with a different payment plan. If they still say no, we transition to a quarter down, with a slightly higher payment plan over time. If they still say no, we shorten the duration of the program and offer just the quarter payment down with no payment plan. If they still say no, then they probably don't trust you and you need to work on sales, but that's beyond this book. But if they still say no, then we would downsell a free trial and put their card on file and get them to commit to consuming our services to increase the likelihood they convert on the back end. And if they still say no, they don't want our services, then to maintain goodwill we offer a complementary nutrition orientation. At that orientation, which might be 24 to 72 hours later, we begin our next series of offers.

Sale #2: Physical Products Sale (Upsell Offer)

At this orientation, after providing some individualized support/value, we would attempt to sell them on a three-month bundle of a full stack of supplements that still help solve their main need…just in a different way. If they said no, we would offer just a one-month supply and put them on a subscription for a discount. If they still said no, we would cross out a handful of the products and just give them the essentials. If they still said no, we would give them the one to two products they absolutely should take. After that, we ask if they need help preparing their food, then we would sell different meal plan prices of a food prep company we had created a relationship with. This helps the customer get results, saves time, and makes us money. Everyone wins.

> ### Pro Tip: Another Example of One-on-One Free Onboarding
>
> The cash I made from the products I sold at orientation covered my payroll to onboard every customer one-on-one. And, my trainers ended up making more per hour than they did taking on personal training clients. So they were happy to do it. My customers loved the added service. *And*, I still made enough profit most times to cover my entire cost of acquisition (advertising, commissions, and payroll) all off of these product sales.
>
> Compare that to the guy down the street always trying to "cut costs" or who is "afraid" of simply making more offers to customers. His employees would make less than mine, so he couldn't keep the best talent. His customers would get worse service and spend less with him, so they'd get worse results. And, he made less money, so he couldn't expand as fast or market to get as many customers. In a competitive market, it's obvious which way of doing business wins in the end. **Bottom line:** People like having problems solved for them in advance, so solve them and profit.

Sales #3: More Services Sale (Continuity)

In the third sale, we are meeting with this customer a few weeks later. We are now positioning this as a "Feedback" meeting. This is how we get valuable feedback about how they are enjoying the service. You should do this for *any* service you have. First, because it gives you valuable information about what you can improve. Second, it allows you to save a customer who is not happy. Third, it provides an upsell opportunity. This is where if the client was having a great time, we would sell them on staying for the long haul. Again, first, we would start with a high ticket prepayment. Then downsell our way to simply closing them on continuity.

If the client is *not* enjoying their time or feel like they need more support, we still naturally sell them a higher level program with *more* support. Every problem is an upsell opportunity. "Oh, you feel like we haven't given you enough support, then how would you like it if we message you every morning and check in with you weekly. Would that help? Awesome. Then I think you'll be a perfect fit for our VIP program. You can start for *free* today, in fact, I'll even credit the entire cost of your first program to the VIP program because you didn't have the best experience…" You get the idea. You just turn around and sell them your next Grand Slam Offer.

Sale #4: Prepay Sale or Last Chance (Up Front Cash, Downsell Continuity)

Finally, the last sale in this four-step sales process is getting them to prepay for services *or* becomes a last chance at getting them on continuity before the end of their treatment plan/program/etc. This helps suck up some of the sales where people "weren't sure" if they wanted to commit yet at the meeting beforehand. You can also use this as an opportunity to upsell those people who committed to continuity on the last example to prepay for a discount. Again, more cash up front.

Weaving Them Together

This may seem like a lot, but done over 6 to 12 weeks, it's not that overwhelming. And communicating with your clients more, will in general, make you more money.

Notice a couple things. First, the big high value offer *is* our Grand Slam Offer. But in the real world, that Grand Slam Offer may have gotten them in the door. Not everyone says yes, so having another Grand Slam Offer in your back pocket will dramatically increase your closing percentage. The second thing to notice is that we still advance *all* prospects to the next stage, even if they said no. This gives us another opportunity to provide value and monetize the person. Do you see how much more effective this is?

Now you may be thinking to yourself…how on earth am I going to do all that? Well, you start by adding one of these conversion opportunities that adds the most money at the lowest cost. Then when you get that down, you add the next one and so forth. Note: prospects *want* you to solve their problem. People *like* buying, they just don't like being *sold*. This is where the Grand Slam Offers come in and make it fun for the buyer and the salesman because everyone likes selling a good deal and everyone likes buying them. A win-win.

Layering these offers together, one at a time, and creating downsells, is what makes your conversion process wildly efficient, not letting a dollar of spending power go to waste.

Four Steps To Picking The Right Offer For Your Money Model

Money models are built off a series of offers. Each offer—or series of offers—satisfies a stage of your Money Models.

We lower CAC. We maximize 30-Day GP. Then, we maximize lifetime GP. And the way I do things, each stage has different offer types that fit that goal. But no matter the type of offer, I follow the same process when adding a new offer to my Money Model. It goes like this: Right stage. Right problem. Right way. Right time.

Right Stage. First, I make sure the offer fits the stage of the Money Model. If I want to get new customers at a reasonable price, I focus on Attraction Offers. If I want to increase 30-Day GP, I add upsells and downsell offers. If I need to maximize lifetime GP, I focus on Continuity Offers. Once I know the offer meets the goal, I move on to the next step.

Right Problem. Customers have many problems. You can't solve them all. So, I prefer to pick problems that make sense for my business, that I can solve with existing resources, and that provide customers big value when solved.

Right Way. Third, I solve based on the customer's preference. Say two people want to lose weight. One might want to change their workouts. The other might want to change their food. You can try to convince people your way is the right way. But most times, they're just gonna go to someone who solves the problem how they want it solved. So, I prefer to present effective options people already want.

Right Time. Fourth, and most importantly, I offer to solve their problem at the right time. Someone might be hungry. But if you ask them if they want another steak after they are full, they'll probably say no. So to sell the most, I make my offer at the time of greatest need.

Summary

First, figure out the stage of your Money Model. Then, make sure your offers fit that stage. Then, make sure your offers solve the right problem for the customer, the way they like it, at the moment they need it the most—*not* when it's convenient for you.

Attraction Offer: Free Presentations

Lost Chapter Author Note: **I ended up cutting this because it got too close to pitching and selling. A book maybe for another time. But this is one of the most widely used ways to get customers. It's not incredibly compelling but it is simple and effective.**

FREE CONSUMPTION TO UPSELL

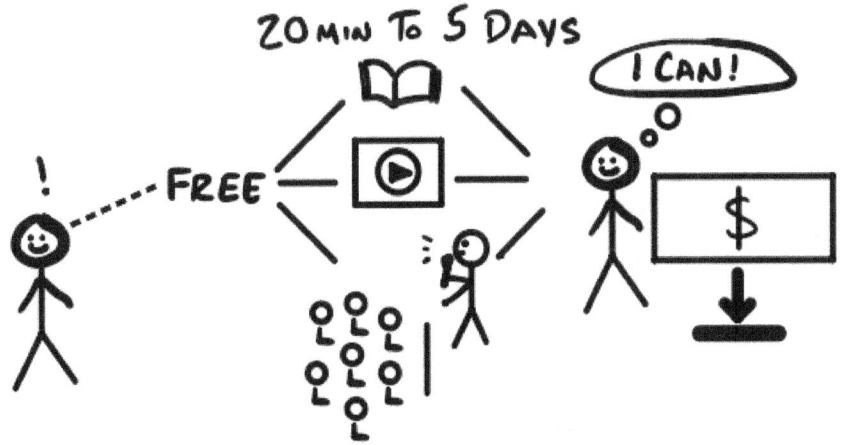

June 2015.

It was a huge marketing conference. I scanned the speaker list and a presentation caught my eye.

"How My Weird Niche Funnel is Making Me $17,137 Per Day…And How You Can Ethically Copy It In Under 10min Or Less"

I didn't have anything to do with gyms, but it looked more interesting than the other options. Besides, if I could find *something* useful in all this marketing stuff, I'd consider it a win. I'd have been thrilled to take home $17,137 a month let alone *per day!* So I went to check it out.

The room was packed to the brim. I barely had room to stand. He started the presentation by dropping a bomb.

"I'm giving away my Ferrari to someone here today. All you have to do is opt-in at this website to find out more."

What!? He made it sound like it was no big deal. It was his Ferrari! *This guy must be legit.*

He then told us about his special money-making websites. He made them in a specific way and put them in a special order to make people buy more of his stuff. Then, he showed us a bit about how to make them for ourselves.

What he did clearly worked. And it made a lot of sense. Too much sense. If I did what he did, I could get what he had. I was sold *before* he even presented an offer.

If he had started with "Hey everyone, come buy my website designer for $2,000," no one would have bought. But sixty minutes in, I bet a third of the room would have taken out their credit cards. I sure would've. That's the power of using presentations to get people to buy your stuff. They work.

Description

Buyers need to know "enough" stuff about your product to buy. And the more expensive or complex the thing, the more information they need. Presentations that educate the audience with the intention of converting them into customers excel at bridging this information gap. They work especially well for complex and expensive stuff for three reasons:

1) **You have a captive audience.**

Presentations require people's attention. So if a person shows up to a presentation, you have a good chance they will pay more attention than they would in other "noisy" advertising environments.

2) **You keep them for a long enough time to explain the thing and provide value.**

Just like presentations require people's attention (and they know it), they also understand that presentations have a time investment. So if a person shows up to a presentation, you have a good chance they'll not only pay more attention, but they'll do it for longer. This makes presentations perfect for making sure leads have all the information they need—you have their attention long enough to actually go through it all.

3) **You make your offer when they're the most motivated to take it.**

A good presentation clarifies the problem they came to solve, what life would be like after your thing solves their problem, how fast and easy it is, showcases loads of people like them who have succeeded with it, and resolves their most common concerns about buying.

By the end, people should see a fast, easy, low-risk way to solve their problems. And at that moment, they will be the most motivated to buy. So that's when we make our offer.

Presentations can last anywhere from 15 seconds to 15 days. The exact length of the presentation matters less, only that the more expensive and more complicated the thing, the longer they tend to get.

For example, when looking at Gym Launch, 78% of customers consumed at least two pieces of "long-form" content before making a purchase. This was a ground-breaking finding. We then reverse-engineered our sales process to *force* people to consume at least two long form pieces of content. This turned "total strangers" into people who wanted to buy our stuff.

This consumption process reverse engineers the trust process to create qualified prospects who are ready to buy. This is the core of marketing: educating a consumer to the point of making a purchasing decision. Sometimes it's a 60-second ad if you're selling a $67 physical product or it's a two-day workshop to sell $100,000 consulting services.

Bottom line: The amount of time you take educating the consumer is directly related to the price and the amount of trust needed. The bigger the plane, the longer the runway has to be in order for the plane to take off. A toy plane can take off in about twenty feet, whereas a 747 "Dreamlifter" needs almost two miles.

Free Education with Offer Examples

Free XYZ Dinner / Free Neuropathy Dinner / Free Diabetic Dinner

Free dinner gets people in the door, and during the meal you make a presentation between 60 and 90 minutes. At the end of the presentation, you make an offer for a product that covers the cost of getting everyone to the dinner. Ideally, more. Of those who buy, you set up individual appointments to offer a much higher ticket item.

Benchmark: Aim to convert a quarter of the room to the lower offer. Of those who take the lower offer, aim to convert at least a third of them to the higher offer. For example, a 100-person audience would have 25 or so people taking the lower offer and eight or so people taking the higher offer.

Free 90-minute Masterclass:

A 90-min presentation structured to break core beliefs around accomplishing their goal. Similar to the dinner option, but you can do it remotely.

<u>Benchmark</u>: Convert 10% of those on the call when an offer is presented.

Free 5 Day Challenge

Give four live 60–90 minute presentations Monday through Thursday. Each presentation covers some useful aspect of the problem they want to solve or result they want to achieve. Then, make your offer on Friday. This works well for converting ice-cold audiences for lower cost and very high-cost offers alike. Each day you would focus your presentation on some core belief that prevents them from buying and, along the way, provide enough useful content they can apply *today* and get value from it *today*.

Example: 5 Day Challenge Ideas For Different Industries:

Entrepreneurship: Free "Find Your Niche" Entrepreneurship Challenge

Real Estate Consulting: Free "Find Your First Real Estate Deal"

Business Flipping Opportunity: Free 5 Day "Buy A Business with $0 Down"

Challenge Sales Consulting: Free 5 Day "Make Your First High Ticket Sale"

Weight Loss: Free 5 Day Plateau Buster

Addiction: Free 5 Days To Freedom Challenge

Pain: Free 5 Day Pain Release Challenge

Life Coach: Free 5 Days to Get Unstuck Challenge

<u>Benchmark</u>: Convert 2 to 5% of people who sign up for the free multi-day challenge.

One of the personal benefits is that you're delivering real value to these people even if they choose not to buy from you. So in the worst case scenario you build goodwill with the marketplace.

Free 3 Day Virtual Summit

Offer: Come see speakers over three full days talk about their topics of expertise. Each topic covers one aspect of (their problem or goal). At the last presentation of the second day and last day and the second presentation of the third day, you offer to help implement the nuggets and strategies covered in the talks. This sets up for the highest ticket offers of all because it has the most possible content for any reasonable person to consume in a row—three full days, for example, Friday midday through Sunday. As a personally surprising finding, the days of the week do not matter. Do them whenever is most convenient for you and your team.

Structure each of the days (4+ presentations) around one of the core beliefs (found below in the pro tips section). Then make a pitch at the end of day two. Repitch on day three. Ending the event with some inspiration to take action tends to work well.

Benchmark: Aim to convert 10% of those attending the final day.

Free Strategy Call

This will typically be "step one" of a two-step sales process which I will cover at depth in a future book (currently unwritten). But fundamentally, you are pitching a value add call, which can act as a pre-qualification call for a later sale. On this call you are triaging to ensure that the person you are on the phone with: 1) Has the budget for what you are selling 2) Has the authority to make a buying decision (or will have those people on the next call) 3) Wants what you are selling 4) Wants to start within the timeframe you deem optimal. The acronym for this is BANT: Budget, Authority, Need, Timing. You provide value on this call by listening and identifying their needs and offering solutions. If they want help with implementation, you can then make them an offer.

Benchmark: Convert 25% of those who make it to the second call.

Pro Tips

Presentations, whether one at 60–90 minutes (like the dinner), or 12+ at 60+ minutes (like the summit) all serve to play on the three core limiting beliefs. The more presentations you have the deeper you can get. Their function stays the same either way.

Three core limiting beliefs:

1) The results must come easy.

2) I must get the best results possible.

3) Results must lead to attention and approval.

1) Results must come easy

- This product is easy to use. This is not frustrating or overwhelming. You can do it.

- This product/service lives up to claims. Here's how the universe will work to help me. It is fair. It will work.

- It was unfair before this because you had an information disadvantage, but now you don't.

- If the universe is unfair, then life is horrible. But the universe will bend to your will now that you have earned it, and you will get status because you deserve it.

2) I must get the best results possible

- If you have messed up in the past, and it's not your fault. It's someone else's or something else's fault.

- Failing would make you feel horrible, which you won't, which means this product is awesome.

3) Results must lead to attention and approval - aka - status

- This product will position you above other people. Here's how you can get everyone to act the way you want to act and be treated the way you want to be treated. External forces will bend to your will.

- If people have not acted the way you wanted in the past, it's not your fault—it's someone else's or something else's fault.

- If people don't do what you want, then they are horrible, but people will, which is why this works.

Anything that will get more people to consume will boost sales. This is why email follow-up, text campaigns, and other participation-based value ads create higher conversion numbers. As a rule to sell by—*the more time they spend with you, the more money they'll spend with you.*

The better the messaging is at aligning and playing to the three core beliefs the better your conversion will get.

Long-form presentation-based selling depends on providing value through entertainment, life lessons, and breaking limiting beliefs. Your focus should be to get them to watch the whole thing, provide value in an entertaining way, and build goodwill. Long-form offers excel at converting cold traffic into buyers. And they work particularly well selling one to many with larger audiences.

Summary

In general, the more expensive the offer, the more audiences want to learn about it before they make a purchase. In general, the colder the audience, the more exposure to a brand, business, or person it takes to build trust. This makes high-ticket offers to cold audiences one of the most difficult things to do in business. To make it work, you have to play the long-game on the front-end. The free education-with-offer forces as much exposure as it can in as short of a window as reasonable.

- Free education, classes, activities, challenges, etc., build goodwill with warmer audiences and trust with colder ones. The more exposure they get the higher ticket your offer can get. The faster they can get the exposure, the sooner you can make the offer with success.

- Long-form methods do a great job at converting cold traffic into buyers and the best job when converting from larger audiences.

- Long-form presentation-based methods focus on providing value through entertainment, life lessons, and touching on limiting beliefs. They aim to retain the audience's attention throughout, deliver value in an engaging way, and build goodwill.

- Presentations, whether single 60–90 minute sessions or multiple hour-long sessions, align with three core limiting beliefs: results must come easy, results must be the best possible, and results must, in some way, lead to attention and approval.

- More and longer presentations delve deeper into these beliefs. It just comes down to keeping engagement during the presentation and maximizing the number of people who show up for the next.

- Follow-up efforts, SMS campaigns, and providing value before and after purchase can increase engagement, show rates, and then conversion rates.

Attraction Offer: Freemium

Lost Chapter Author Note: **I ended up cutting this because I didn't think it applied to enough businesses. But if you have a software or media business (any business that has close to 100% incremental margins) this is a dangerous but effective money model used by billion dollar companies.***

I learned this by studying how freemium software companies upsold me. That being said, almost every one of the companies listed in the examples section has funding. If you do not have investors and *large* amounts of capital, I would *not* recommend this structure.

That being said, I am including it as a way of presenting a complete picture of possible approaches. If you have something incredibly valuable—so valuable that lots of people come towards you without marketing—then you have something that qualifies for this structure. Otherwise, steer clear.

Description

Freemium is one of the most dangerous acquisition strategies, but also can be one of the most powerful. This is definitely an advanced move. To be honest, I've seen it done incorrectly by really smart people more times than I've seen it done correctly. One of the key points to understand about freemium is that it is *not* a business model, it is an acquisition strategy. That's a *very* important distinction.

The idea is, you give something away that is so valuable that people come to get it and *continually use it* for free. They must come from word of mouth because the product is so good. It must cost $0 to get them to use it (or just enough advertising to get it going so it then spreads virally). That is where this gets tricky.

Examples

Dropbox (Online Storage)

Free storage…up to a point. Then after that, you pay.

Spotify (Free Music App)

Free music forever, with ads. Remove ads for a fee.

Wistia (Video Hosting)

Free video uploads. After a certain amount you need to pay more.

Gmail storage

Free email. After a certain period, upgrade for more inbox space or start having your emails deleted. Fear of loss makes you upgrade.

Details

Here's what it looks like when done right: You give away a core piece of software that provides value to someone's life or business. They don't value it enough to pay for it, but if it's free they will use it *continually*. This means you get hundreds, or thousands, or hundreds of thousands of people coming to you…for free. Ad spend: $0.

The idea is to *then* use your marketing and sales team to make offers to these "customers" to upsell them into higher levels of service. This gives your sales team a pool of "free leads" to upsell. It's always easier to upsell someone than to sell them. Designing this can be incredibly challenging. You must give something away that 1) costs you almost nothing to fulfill, 2) provides *continuous value* (not one-time), and 3) doesn't give away so much of the farm that they'll never want to buy something else. A very difficult balance.

In businesses selling to businesses, one of the key ways of doing this is giving something away that exposes a hole in their business, something that your next paid product solves.

In a business selling to consumers, this typically comes in the form of giving away something people use. At the same time, it limits their use in some way that anyone who would regularly use it would need more of. Either through advertising or limits that once they start using it, they would want to increase.

You'll notice this play works well with software because software is 1) virtually free for each additional user and 2) intended to provide continuous value. So the "only" part you have to nail is how much and exactly what to give away (which is still very hard).

Your true cost of acquisition when using this model is understanding what percentage of free customers upgrade, and determining your cost of servicing a free customer. So, for example, if it costs you .05/mo to service a free customer, and you upsell 1% of customers, then your cost of acquisition is .05/mo divided by .01 = $5/mo. As long as your average revenue per paid user is $15/mo+ you'll have a profitable business that could grow. Because, again, remember that you still have costs of doing business before you start to profit.

Here's what it looks like when done wrong: You give away your core thing. People use it for free. Then they don't want to buy your next thing. Now you are just running a business that loses money servicing customers for free.

> **Roadblocks**
>
> Here are just a handful of the problems you can encounter with this model.
>
> #1 Conversion Problem: Conversion percentage from free to paid is too low.
>
> #2 Value Problem: You give away something that people don't find valuable enough to tell other people about. You spend money marketing your free thing, and still people don't want to tell enough people about it for you to be profitable.
>
> #3 Cost Problem: People want it. They tell their friends about it, but your costs of fulfilling them for free are too high relative to what you make from paid customers. So you are not profitable.

Summary Points

Overall, freemium is a very hard strategy to get right. It's also something that can be very powerful. If it's your first rodeo, and you don't know everything there is to know about a freemium acquisition strategy, then I would definitely *not* recommend it.

This is a billion dollar strategy that I mostly included for completeness. I think you need to be a seasoned pro and know your numbers like you know your children's names. If you can nail it, though, you can get unlimited free leads and viral growth as a result.

It's important to remember that this isn't a business model. It's an acquisition strategy. It has to be free and valuable enough to spread, but not so valuable that customers use it without upgrading. If you use this strategy, good luck! You're a smarter man/woman than I am.

Attraction Offer: Free Pick Your Price

Lost Chapter Author Note: ***I removed this upsell because I thought some businesses might lose money doing it since they wouldn't be able to close the upsell that makes this profitable. But with skill, it's a great goodwill play that also makes money and generates leads.***

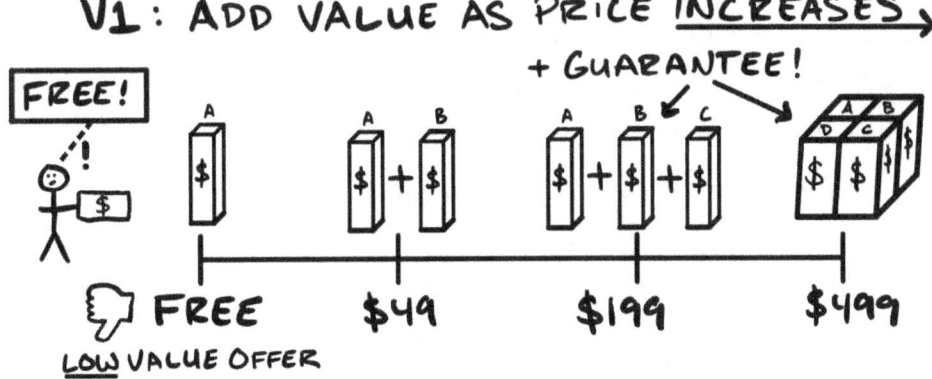

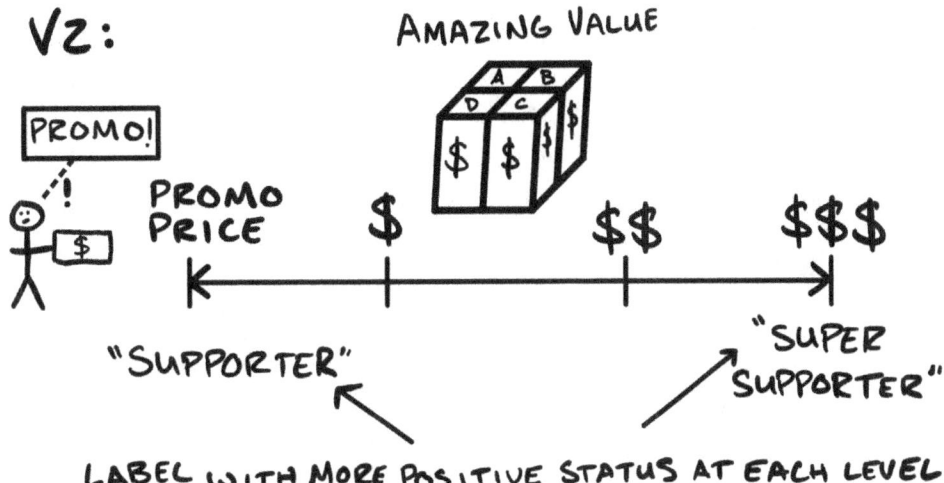

June 2020. Austin, Texas.

I could see the Texas heat bouncing off the hood of the car as we drove. The roads were empty, not a car in sight. It was like driving through a ghost town, except the town was our home. It was in the thick of the COVID-19 lockdowns. As Leila and I were driving back from the pharmacy for some goods, we saw a young girl on the side of the road frantically waving a sign.

Free Car Wash

Intrigued, I said "I wonder what the deal is. There's gotta be something to it. Wanna go check it out?"

Leila obliged my whim, as she had many times in the past. She knew just how much I love going through sales processes. So I turned the wheel of the car toward the girl and headed up the ramp next to her. Around the bend, we rolled our car into the main car wash lane. As we pulled up, a man stood up from his seat in the shade. We came to a stop and rolled down the window. He pointed at the pricing chart and exhaled his spiel, which it became clear he had already done hundreds of times already that day.

"The standard wash is 100% free but we're accepting donations on behalf of the staff to help the guys feed their families and get through this. We would all be very appreciative. We accept cash, credit, and Venmo." Then he shut up, and said nothing.

I got the hint and took out a twenty dollar bill. Looking at the pricing board, it was more expensive than the most expensive automated wash they charged for even during normal conditions. He grabbed the twenty, and gave me a ticket and waved me on.

I'm always pro-business, and always will be. I felt great about helping a group of working men out. That being said, it had a very different feel than any normal purchase. Normally we buy things and don't think much past the transaction. In this instance, my purchase was funding something great—the American dream. As we went through the wash line, I couldn't shut up about it.

"How great was that!? Goodwill. Lots of new business. Cash flow on a high margin service. Brilliant. I'm definitely figuring out a version of this for the gyms."

And in the middle of COVID, our gyms began using this scripting in their sales process and it worked wonderfully. People who couldn't normally close were able to get an average ticket of about $99 which is more than the average low barrier offer. It was splendid. I'll give you the details about how to do it below and how you can apply an offer like this to attract new customers.

Description

You market the promotional offer as free. When the person gets to the checkout, you give them an offer to pick their own price. You will explain the benefits of investing more equating to higher investment in their own results. If they're after results, the more they pay, the more they will pay attention.

Examples

Lemonade Stand

Offer: Free Lemonade Cup

Upsell: But you can choose to pay something to help the families of the employees. As an additional bonus, the crew offered to make a cup of hand-squeezed lemonade for anyone who pays over $5 and give you a pitcher to take home with you for any donation over $25, and give you three months of shipments for anything over $99+.

Car Wash

Offer: Free Machine Car Wash Water & Soap

Upsell: But you can choose to pay something to help the families of the employees. As an additional bonus, the crew offered to wax anyone's car who pays over $30 and hand buff anyone over $67, and do the entire interior of the car for anything over $99+.

Weight Loss

Offer: Free 21-Day Weight Loss

Upsell: Pick your price, most people pay $99. We give this just to the coaches and their families. If you pick $99 we'll give you an extra 1–1 call. If you pay over $199 we will also provide our entire supplement handbook. If you pay $499 we will guarantee you will lose 10lbs, and if you don't, we will let you use that as credit towards any service we have.

Dentist

Offer: Free Dental Cleaning

Upsell: Pick whatever you want to pay. Most people pay $99 which also gets them an extra YY or $299 for an extra VWZ.

Coaching

Offer: Free Coaching/Mentorship

Upsell: Pick your price. If you pay $299 you will also get the course that goes with it. At $997 you get 6 group calls on top of this. The $0 price comes only with access to the group.

> ## Free Versus Discount Note
>
> This offer does not work with a discount wrapper

Details

To further incentivize them paying, you offer bonuses for three levels of payment (think small, medium, large) to encourage them to pay something more than $0. Ultimately, if someone doesn't want to pay for the first thing, you must give them the basic level for free. That being said, you can and should still upsell them on other products and services during their time with you.

This is similar to a limited free offer except instead of "either or," you have a sliding scale with no predetermined amounts, only rungs. It also has no max. People can pay whatever they want.

You want to make sure that at the beginning of the sale you explain that you do have a pick-your-price type setup and that the staff is offering different "bonuses" at different levels, but they are not obligated to pay anything. It'll seem like they are paying the employees, not the business, which for some reason people feel better about (even though businesses pay employees…sigh).

Explaining that you are accepting donations/allowing people to pick their own price will avoid any awkwardness at the end. You also get the goodwill of the prospect by being up front.

When selling with that pre-frame, though, you can and should hit the prospect hard with confrontational questions to ensure they would be a good long-term candidate. If you feel as though they have no intention of staying ongoing in any service that you have, *weed them out*. Be genuine about this. This should feel like an interview. The types of clients you want are the ones who willingly pay and are appreciative. This is sort of a mini-test for that. Ask real questions to gauge commitment level for their own good and yours. Examples: *Are you willing to change the way you do X? Are you willing to stop doing Y? What if life gets busy, will you stop showing up? Will you attend all of these appointments?*

Make sure that the thing you are giving away for free has low operational costs so you can still give it to people without burning out your staff. Save the higher operational cost stuff for the people who choose to pay.

After you get to the end of the pitch, you will outline what they get at each level, then say "we accept Visa, Mastercard, or XYZ payment, which would you prefer to use?" Then shut up. They will take out their card and tell you what level they want. It's hard for people to say no.

Summary Points

These offers can generate a lot of goodwill when done properly. People feel good when they buy them because it is not a demand, it is a choice. It pulls on people's generosity. People feel 100% in control of their own destiny, and you can play up the fact that you are helping folks for free. It sets up a relationship based on goodwill and sets the stage for future upsells. On top of that, the conversion rate is very high, although the ticket average is typically lower with this type of play. It works well in low-trust environments because it has so much goodwill loaded into it. It is one of the easier "free upsells" that exist.

Pro Tip: PAID VERSION of "Pick Your Price"

I saw an art gallery use the play this way: *every piece of art had a price range.* They said people could choose how much they wanted to support the artist. For example, "this painting is between $149 and $299". I asked the owner how it worked. She told me most people pay more than the halfway point because they don't want to seem cheap or unsupportive. This version is half goodwill, half capitalism. I like it. Give it a try if it fits your business.

Upsell Offer: Free With Alternate Revenue Stream

Lost Chapter Author Note: **I removed this upsell because I didn't think enough businesses would be able to use it. That being said, it does crush!***

FREE WITH 2ND REVENUE STREAM

FREE + $

YOU GET THIS VALUABLE THING OTHERS CHARGE FOR **FREE** FOREVER AS LONG AS YOU...

- KEEP PAYING FOR THIS ONE...
- BUY THE OTHER THING YOU NEED NEXT FROM **US**...
- LET US USE THIS VALUABLE RESOURCE YOU HAVE ACCESS TO...

2019ish.

The following is a rough paraphrasing from a story a gym owner told me that taught me: 1) an excellent downsell/upsell strategy, and 2) a really nice way to graciously exit anyone from a sales conversation who doesn't want to buy your main product.

When someone walks in, tours the place, and says no to joining—which used to kill me—I had this realization. Instead of awkwardly escorting them out of my gym, why not offer them something free instead? Instead, I say, "No worries," and hand them a USB drive. "Here's everything you need to do this program from home, absolutely free."

You should see their faces. In this industry where everyone's trying to lock you into contracts, they think I'm some kind of saint. But here's the real move—after I give them the USB, I simply add:

"To get you a head start, let's book you for a nutrition orientation so you can see the results you want. The orientation is on us. We just want to get this community healthy, and maybe when you can afford it, you'll think of us."

Almost 100% of the people who said no to my gym membership end up in these nutrition orientations. And guess what? During these orientations, we sell them supplements instead of workout programs.

The crazy part? These people who initially rejected working out spend 50% more on supplements than my regular clients. I've basically created a "no prospect left behind" approach, and my sales team loves it because they help everyone who walks in.

Everyone around here calls it "the no sale sale". Perfect name, right? I'm selling to people who think they aren't buying anything.

And once I started doing that, I thought to myself, "why not offer this free USB as my front end just to get people in? Then I can upsell them an in-person version for money - or - they can keep buying supplements from us every month and not even use up gym space. Win-win." So, that's what I did. And, it worked.

***

It goes to show that people want the *same* problem solved in *different* ways. Offering multiple ways to solve their problem gives you a few more at-bats. What's more, this strategy allowed him, and the gyms who subsequently modeled it in our community, a way to turn *every single prospect into a sale*.

There are a few ways to use it, so let's dive in. As a downsell, like in the story. Or, as a primary offer, which he alludes to at the end. We'll dive into both.

Description

This is an offer that depends strongly on the types of monetization/revenue streams available to a business. In the simplest terms, we are providing one type of service (or product) for free, and upselling something else.

You can upsell something as a one-time service or product to offset advertising costs. Or, you can make the upsell recurring. Or you can plan your entire business around giving one thing away for free and monetizing with another. It works for one-time services or even recurring services, provided the alternative revenue stream has sufficiently high margins to afford both fulfillment types. But most variations chunk up to two larger buckets:

Paired Upsell: I give you thing A for free, in exchange for buying thing B.

OR

Independent Upsell: I give you thing A for free, and I will encourage you to buy thing B.

Those are all slightly nuanced ways of expressing the same concept/offer. But they will hopefully generate some different ideas for you on how to use this in your business or your clients' businesses.

Examples

Storage

Offer: You get a free month of storage.

Paired Upsell: Do you want to buy a lock for your storage unit? (The only locks that fit our doors are the ones we sell and cannot be purchased anywhere else).

Weight Loss Clinic

Offer: Free 28-Day Program

Independent Upsell: (At nutrition orientation—kickoff of program after first sign up). You're going to want this $400 supplement package to get the best results for the free 28 days of service.

Physical Therapist

Offer: 4 Free Treatments

Independent Upsell: You're going to need these orthotics, bands, braces, oils, and athletic tape, to maximize the effectiveness of the treatment.

Info/Coaching/Education + Software

Offer: I will coach you for free indefinitely on your agency as long as you use our software.

Paired Upsell: We monetize inherently on the software.

Real Example: Free Book on Real Estate

Upsell #1: Shipping cost

Upsell #2: Audio version

Upsell #3: Deal contract templates

Upsell #4: Where to find deals—training

Upsell #5: How to find financing if you have no money

Note: Each of these things are necessary requisites for being successful using the strategies outlined in the book. The hardest sale is the first sale—the opportunity vehicle—the book. The rest of the upsells are the things they will need along the journey.

Free Versus Discount Note

This works with a discount wrapper. "You can get service from us for only $5/mo (normally $100/mo) as long as you continue to use our products."

An acquaintance of mine who owned a very successful chain of 200+ weight loss clinics grew it on this simple offer. They offered $5 per month of weight loss services for a year *if and only if* the client used their supplements, bars, shakes, and meal program. Their guarantee was also contingent on this continued usage/purchasing.

They were a successful business and employed doctors and nurses at the facilities, but despite this, gave their service away because they made so much on their consumable products. This gave me an interesting insight—people were more willing to pay for the products than they were for the service from white-coated medical professionals. People *love* tangible goods. Something I always try to incorporate with services if I can find a convenient way.

Details

You'll want to use a multi-step sales process with this offer. If you are marketing "thing A" for *free*, then you must be able to give it away for free. So it is key that you give away something that has low incremental costs (i.e., adding another unit doesn't cost much).

If you are using it as a front-end offer, you want to make the next thing you are selling/upselling them to be the next natural thing that the prospect would need. It is key to understand your prospect's problem and the solutions available better than they do. That is where good money model design becomes paramount.

In the examples I gave, the money model does not end there. There are still more upsells that will occur in each of these scenarios:

- Storage will upsell boxes, larger storage units, and commitment.

- Weight loss clinic will upsell continuity of service, continuity of supplements, done-for-you meals, bars, hormone treatment, etc. They'll also likely close a card for continuity of service so the free service is also a Free Trial + Penalty. This way you are capturing multiple streams of revenue.

- Physical therapists will probably upsell a long-term treatment program bundle.

The effectiveness of this play is based on:

1) The prospect's perception of how essential/required the next thing is (like the lock in the storage unit scenario).

2) How seamless the upsell process is for the prospect. If you make it frictionless, you can get 90% plus take rates on upsells for these offers. They should *feel* like it makes *total sense* to buy it.

The biggest benefit to using this offer as a free front end is being able to liquidate acquisition cost. If you make $0 on the free thing (naturally), but you know 80% take a $300 upsell with 80% margins, then you know you are making $300 x 80% x 80% = $192 *per* free thing given away…and that's just the first upsell. There will and should be many others.

But since the take rate is so high, and it is up front, this is one of the *easiest* ways to generate cash up front with little to no operational drag. Physical and digital products pair very well with services for this specific money model.

We use this all the time for internal stuff. What I mean is using it to market to an existing audience. You can encourage them to bring friends for the free thing. They will be excited to do that and to participate. So it will end up generating new customers and revenue with an easy offer. Basically, this combines a free trial with an upsell. Since most of your clients take the offer, in many cases you can make more money going free + upsell than selling a moderately priced thing up front. Consider meeting with 100 folks and selling 30 people a $99 thing versus meeting with the same 100 folks and selling all 100 a free thing, then upselling 80 of them on the $300 products. You end up with more money *and* more customers (plus the referrals).

You can obviously use this up front. With cold traffic, you're going to want to close a trial + credit card on the first transaction, then upsell product on the second, otherwise you will get a lot of no-shows.

NOTE: If someone does not buy the upsell, they are unlikely to stay. It's the greatest predictor of back-end conversion. So although that sale may seem minor, it's the most important for the long-term value of the customer. You must focus on it. It's not a nice-to-have. It's a *must-have*.

Summary Points

Great internal play to your audience. Generates lots of referrals. Easy to sell. Pair it with a free trial for cold traffic so you can assume the back-end continuity and far better back-end conversion. Can generate more cash than selling something low(ish) ticket. Almost always gets a lot of volume in the door.

Continuity Offer: Lifetime Upgrades

Get Them To Stick

Lost Chapter Author Note: ***This chapter delineates lifetime versus one-time bonuses. I thought too many people would struggle to fit it into their business. But if you have a continuity service business, this model can be very effective.***

Version 1:

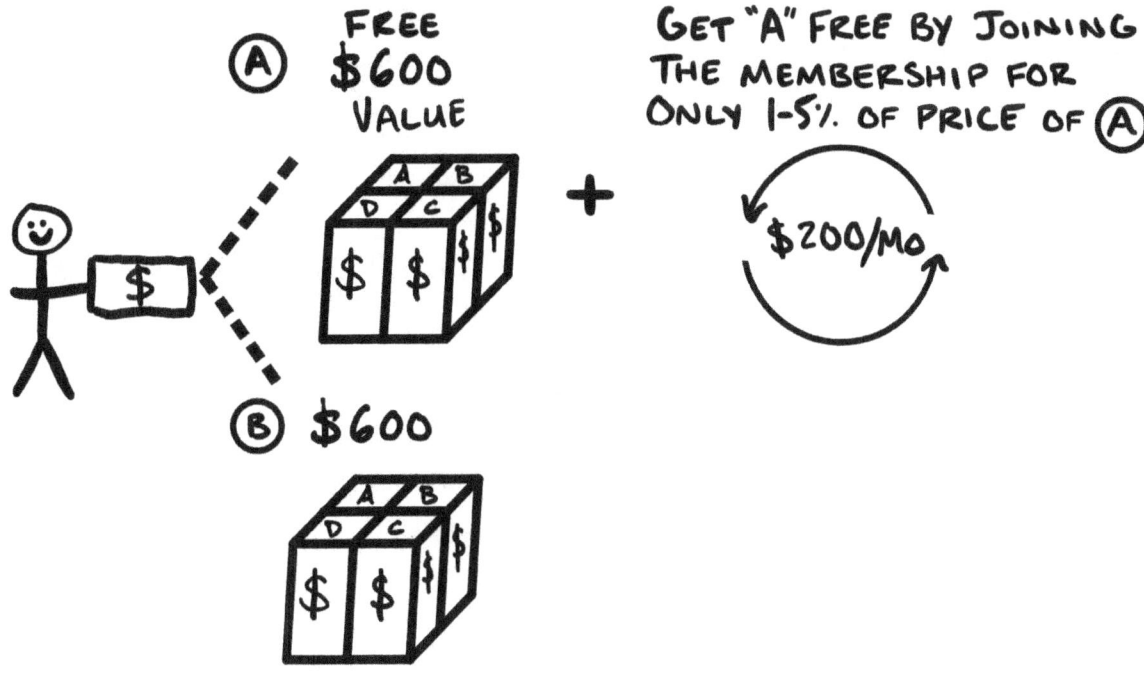

Version 2:

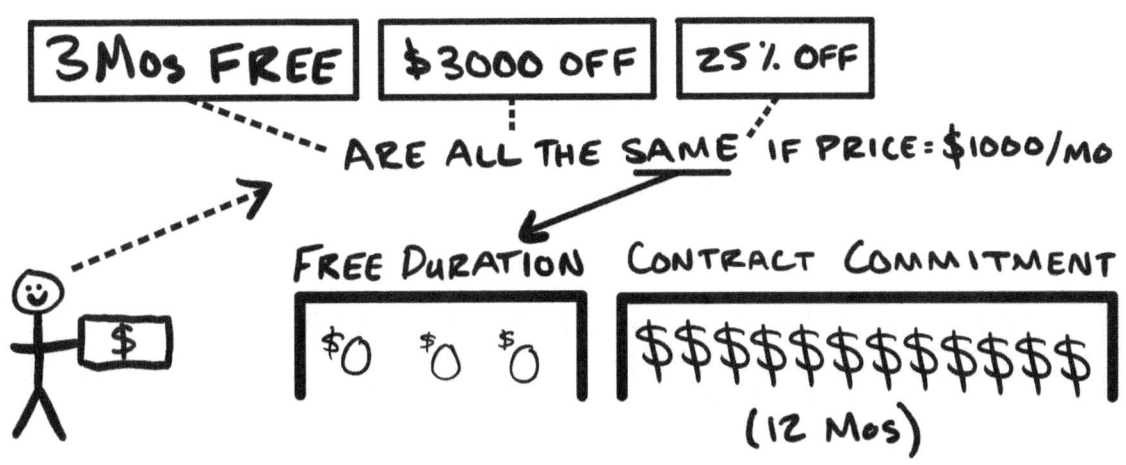

June 2017.

After launching 36 gyms by hand and getting absolutely crippled by payment processing problems (crazy story by the way—you can read all about it in *$100M Leads*), Leila and I had enough. We wanted to wind down Gym Launch and do a weight loss offer instead. But that meant I had lots of gyms to break the news to. And when I called up the first gym to cancel his launch—*he refused!* After some back and forth, he asked if I would just teach him instead of flying out to do the launch. I agreed. Gym Launch was saved. And, just like that, I stumbled on the Gym Launch licensing offer we still use today.

So instead of flying out, I provided our already-proven Gym Launch-ing stuff. Think ads, scripts, sales training, follow-up tactics and so on—and I licensed it all for $16,000. The stuff worked. Gyms using our materials made *on average ~$30,000*—almost twice their investment—*in their first 30 days.* For the average gym owner, that was *life-changing.* But I still had a looming problem.

Even though the product was expensive and worked, I could only sell each customer *once.* So after I sold it, that was it. A problem if you want to reinvest in growth *and* pay yourself (my preference, I like getting paid). So to solve it, I had to sell something else. A continuity product fit the bill.

Even if I used *all* of the cash from the first purchase to get more customers, the continuity offer would keep money coming in. *But, I didn't have a continuity product.* Boo. Then, I had a stroke of luck. A gym reached out and gave me the perfect opportunity…

"Hey man how are you d-"

"I'm in."

"Uh…on what?"

"Seriously? On your next thing. I've already made $55k in the last 6 weeks—a *340% return.* So if your next thing is half as good as this, let me buy it yesterday."

Gotta think fast. "So, uh, how's your semi-private training going?"

"Huh, we actually don't have any." he replied.

"…how much do you make on supplements?"

"Zero. We don't do that either."

Feeling confident now. "What about churn? Hiring? Internal plays? You got those sorted?"

"Uhh…not really." His confidence dropping. Wind coming out of his sales.

Time for the offer. "I see. So…do you want to get out of the daily grind and *actually* scale a legit chain of gyms?"

He puffed back up. "Dude, that sounds awesome! Like I said—whatever you got, I'm in!"

Downselling the upsell. "Alright. It's a way higher price and you gotta stay longer, cool?"

"I think so," he said. *Getting a bit shaky.*

"It's…" punching numbers into my calculator. "…$42,000 per year. For three years."

He sat there. Silent.

Shoot. Throw in the bonus. "And on top of that—you'll get access before you start paying, cool?"

Taking out his own calculator, he looked shocked, then smirked. "Alex, that's $3,200 per month. That's 20% cheaper monthly than Gym Launch. You got a deal. What do I get first?"

Oh boy… "Well, that depends on what's holding back your gym right now. So we'll figure out the bottleneck, then I'll make you a play that'll solve it. We'll repeat that process every two weeks until you've got more money than you know what to do with. Sound good?"

"Bi-weekly plays—*specific* to my gym? Fantastic. Let's do it!"

***

Little did he know. I had nothing ready—yet. I left that up to future Alex. But, I did know one thing. I had a continuity offer. One where I provided a new money-making play *every fourteen days.* Yikes.

It was insane. And so were the results. I would keep this up for almost two years. It exhausted me to my core. But, it meant I could plow all the extra cash into getting more customers *and* get paid. So I did. And Gym Launch's revenue went up *more than 13X.* From ~$300,000 per month to ~$4,000,000+ per month as a result. So…uh…it worked.

This turned into an important lesson for me. Customers would start any offer if I made it tasty enough. But, they'd only stick if they had good reasons to. So I gave them one…*every 14 days.* Our revenue kept scaling. Not because we sold more customers, but *because I gave them good reasons to* keep paying. So, a good offer got them to start, and good bonuses got them to stick.

Now, so can yours.

Description

With the previous offers in this section, we got people to *start* our continuity program. Now, we focus on getting them to *stick*. So once they become customers—they *stay* customers.

That said, we can get people to stick to continuity offers longer with bonuses. More value *on top of* the continuity product itself. So improving monthly stick means providing extra value, in some way, monthly.

When I make a bonus, I think of "when" and "what". For the "when" part, I use <u>delays</u> or <u>milestones</u>. This means *how long they have to wait* (delays) or *what they have to do or achieve* (milestones) to get the thing.

For the "what," I give them a <u>one-time bonus</u>, a <u>variable bonus</u>, or a <u>lifetime upgrade</u>. A one-time bonus, you give *one time*. Think of one thing, one use, one activity, or one-time access. A variable bonus, you give on a schedule, but it changes each time. And a lifetime upgrade means a permanent high-value change in continuity status—think an entire feature or service.

This means that you simply pair a "when" with a "what". Putting them together, the person has to wait a certain period or do certain stuff to get the bonus once, get a variable bonus on a schedule (like monthly, quarterly, yearly, etc.), or get the same bonus forever. The time to the first bonus extends their stay one-time. And if you keep giving them bonuses, you can extend their stay more times.

If you're not sure what bonus to offer, I think of it in two ways. First, how can I give them more or better of something. From a value equation perspective, think faster, easier, risk free. And finally, if you just want a list of different types of bonuses, refer to: Bonuses Chapter in *$100M Offers* - and - Feature Downsells in *$100M Money Models*. Both will give you different perspectives on types of bonuses.

All in all, you can probably make a continuity offer on anything that provides continuous value. You can get them to stick to that continuity offer longer by adding bonus value well after their first payment, and often.

Examples

Delayed One-Time Bonus—Local Service

When: Stay a recurring customer for four months in a row and you become an "advanced member"

What: Get Access to Our Annual Customer Appreciation Palooza

Delayed Recurring Bonus—Local Service

When: Stay a recurring customer for four months in a row and on the fifth month…

What: VIP First-in-Line Access to In-Demand Timeslots

Milestone Bonus—Digital Product

When: For every friend you refer

What: We give you one more module

Recurring Bonus—Consumable Physical Product

When: Stay a recurring dog food customer

What: A new dog treat/toy/book every month

When: Stay a recurring butcher box meat customer

What: Lifetime free bacon with every order (if you cancel, you lose it)

Continuous Use Physical Use: Car Lease

When: Every 3,000 miles (milestone) or every six months (delay)

What: You can get the car serviced free (bonus)

Important Notes

Make sure customers know about your bonuses. They can only get excited enough to stay longer to get it *if they know it exists.* So tell them! Whether they're just signing up, or a year in, always let them know what comes *next.* And—if you have recurring bonuses—right after you give it to them, let them know about the *next one.* Always keep 'em wanting more.

How to tell customers about upcoming bonuses. Let customers know the <u>type</u> of bonus they get, but keep the bonus itself a surprise. This gives you flexibility *and* makes the bonus more valuable. In the Gym Launch example, customers knew they would get a new play from me every month. But I kept the exact play a surprise. To be clear, the bonus was *on top of licensing stuff they already got.* This made it both recurring and valuable. Which makes sense because we want them to pay as much as possible *continuously.*

Variable bonuses or Lifetime Upgrades. Unless your bonus gives a huge and permanent improvement, keep it variable. No matter how good you make your thing, customers will get used to it. So giving new stuff more often (even if less valuable) frequently keeps more customers interested longer.

Making milestones for your milestone bonuses. As always, I try to make all my milestones either: things that make my customer more successful—think activation points. Or, things that make me successful—advertising on my behalf. Ideally, things that do both. For example, if publicly posting that they are starting a weight loss challenge will increase their adherence *and* advertise my business—then why not give them a bonus when they do it? Think of all the tips from the Win Your Money Back Chapter in *$100M Money Models*, all those apply.

Combine bonuses when you can. You can combine both the "whens" and the "whats" from earlier. For the "whens," you can have something that they get at a delay <u>and</u> another bonus they get only if they achieve a milestone. For the "whats," a one-time bonus will get them to sign up and stay to that point. A recurring bonus (variable or lifetime upgrade) will keep them staying after. So you might put one big bonus for getting them to stay for X period, then another permanent upgrade after they get to Y period, and another one-time bonus after they achieve a milestone. Use 'em all.

With proper framing, you can make lots of stuff a variable bonus. The bonuses can be new things, better things *updates*, or more of what they already like. Giant streaming services do all three. They already have more stuff than any one person could ever consume. Ever. But they still come out with new shows, more seasons of shows that people like, and better ways to match content to viewers' preferences.

Give customers status and bragging rights when they unlock bonuses. Once customers unlock a big bonus, change their label. For instance, after someone stays six months, you might go from calling them a customer to a "VIP". Smart cookies like us align the label with traits of loyal customers. From a customer to "committed," "lifer," "advanced," "invested," "all-in," "elite," and so on. Bonus points if you make the label something they can brag about *and* feel bad about losing. Kinda like airlines with their super duper diamond status.

Celebrate status changes publicly. The more you can pair status changes with little ceremonies or graduations—the more value the status change has. The more status they gain, and the more the status gets them, the less they'll want to lose it. And—by extension—getting them to *stick*. You can do these as monthly, quarterly, or when you have big achievements to celebrate.

Summary Points

- To get more people to stick for the long term, give them bonuses over the long term.

- When making bonuses you want to know the "when" and "what".

- "When" you give a bonus is either on a delay or from a milestone.

- Delayed bonuses you give after a specified number of payments or time has passed.

- Milestone bonuses you give after the customer does something or achieves a result.

- "What" type of bonus you give: one-time, variable, and lifetime upgrades.

- One-time bonuses happen once and extend the duration of a customer's tenure *once*. So, you may need to give lots of one-time bonuses over time to keep them staying… over time.

- Variable bonuses give a different thing each time.

- Lifetime upgrade bonuses give additional features or services.

- You can combine bonuses. The more incentives someone has to start and stick, the better.

- When somebody earns a big bonus, give them a new label to show their superior status.

- Make the bonus a big deal to the customer—and do it in public if they feel OK with it.

Continuity Offer: Lifetime Discounts

Get Them To Stick

Lost Chapter Author Note: **This chapter delineates lifetime versus one-time discounts. It was in an earlier version of* $100M Money Models, *but I cut it out since I think a lot of people would cut their prices too much and ultimately damage their business.* **

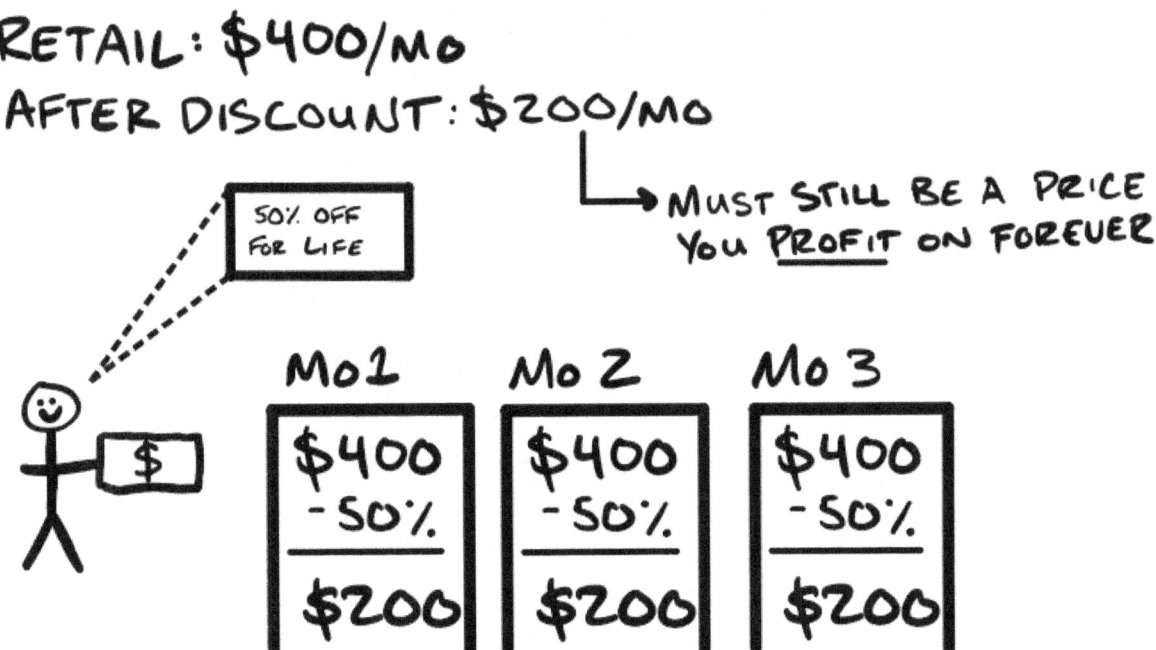

Summer 2015.

My phone rang. Catching a glimpse of the ID, I saw "The Opener". I had tried for weeks to get a hold of this guy. I didn't know much about him. But, a business friend of mine said if I wanted to take launching gyms seriously, I should talk to the best. And "The Opener" was the best.

When big chains open a new store, they send their "all-star team". Their best marketers, their best operators, their best product people, and so on. This ensures that when the store opens up, it makes an *amazing* first impression in that market. Right up my alley. And *when* the business establishes itself, the all-stars hire their replacements. Then, they rinse and repeat.

"The Opener" opened gyms for a billion-dollar gym franchise. So I couldn't wait to learn from him. We spoke for almost an hour. I learned a lot from him and this gold nugget topped it off:

"We open every location with 400+ recurring members, or we don't open," he said.

"You can't be serious."

"No man, for real. We *crush* grand openings."

"What do you do?"

"We advertise a 14-day trial into a lifetime discount on their membership. But we only offer the lifetime discounts to the members who sign up *before we open*. We call it the 'founding member discount.' And since the discount lasts for life, and there's a short time to get it, a lot of people want it. So we open up packed."

Woah. "How on earth do you stay profitable with *lifetime* discounts?"

"We know our numbers—after the 14-day trial 80% sign up. So if we get 500 trials, 400 bill on day 15. We turn a profit in month one. Better yet, most of them stick because they don't want to lose their lifetime discount. So they become lifetime customers."

It made too much sense. Not only was this a strong attraction offer, it also got people to stick for the long term. He had just given me a billion dollar secret.

Description

Lifetime Discount offers, at least the way I use them, give customers a cheaper price *as long as they stay on recurring payments.* Customers get incentivized to take the offer now because they get value at a discount *now*. And with the way I use Lifetime Discounts, customers also stick because if they leave, *they can't get it back.*

To make Lifetime Discounts even more attractive, add urgency (limited time), scarcity (limited number) and believable reasons for both (ex: grand opening).

If you add these components, the Lifetime Discounts work like magic. Just offer to discount somebody's monthly rate so long as they pay it. Make it more attractive by limiting the number of buyers or the amount of time they buy it. There you have it. (To learn more about urgency and scarcity refer to the Urgency and Scarcity Chapters in *$100M Offers*).

A Lifetime Discount only works if you actually charge more when this offer ends. Otherwise you just list the price and "pretend" it's a discount. Gross.

The Opener used Lifetime Discounts as an attraction offer. I prefer to use them as upsells. I let people keep a "Rollover Upsell" discount *only* if they finish out the credited payments. This gets them to *buy* <u>and</u> gets them to *stick*. Think of it like "price protection" where you keep it so long as you keep paying for it.

Final point: when giving Lifetime Discounts or any other discount, make sure you make a profit after the discount.

<u>Examples</u>

<u>Recurring Local Service</u>:

Retail Price: $400/mo

Offer: 50% off retail for life

Discount Price: $200/mo

Reason: New location

Urgency: Until we open

Scarcity: Classes fill up!

<u>Digital Product Development: Early Access</u>

Retail: $39/mo

Offer: $20 off retail for life

Discount Price: $19/mo

Reason: It will have bugs

Urgency: Until we launch it

Scarcity: Only wanna take on X to get feedback

<u>Recurring Physical Product: New Supplements Flavor "Tester" Pricing</u>

Retail: $19.99/mo

Offer: $14.99/mo for life

Discount Price: $14.99/mo

Reason: We want your feedback!

Urgency: Until X date

Scarcity: Until we run out of this batch

<u>ALTERNATE: Recurring Physical Product: New Supplements Flavor "Tester" Pricing</u>

Retail: $19.99/mo

Offer: $5 off per month for life after you stay for five months

Discount: $14.99/mo

Reason: We want to reward your loyalty/commitment

Urgency: None

Scarcity: None

Important Notes

Lifetime Discounts come with a big fat warning: *know your numbers.* Lifetime Discounts work pretty good. So if you don't know your numbers, you can get into serious trouble. This offer gives customers a locked-in discount *so long as they pay.* So remember, the cost of getting customers and the cost of delivering *will* change. If those costs get higher than your profit, and they have a locked-in rate, *you've got problems.*

Three ways to display your lifetime discount. You can offer a percentage off retail (50% off), a dollar amount off retail ($20 off), or a fixed price (price protection). The first two are far more flexible. If things change (they always do), you can adjust your retail price and lifetime discount customers *still keep their discount.* So if you decide to offer a fixed price for life—<u>know your numbers</u>.

Limit price protection for fixed periods. I try to always give myself flexibility. Giving one price *forever* limits me. To reconcile that, I offer price protection for a *period of time* rather than *forever.*

Ex: Normally $50/mo but you can pay $20/mo for the next 36 months.

Never waste a crisis. Lifetime discounts are almost too good to be true. So you need an equally strong reason to make it seem believable. The *best* ones are real and true life events. Just as much as you can give a discount because something good happened, you can give a discount because something bad happened. Here are a few of my favorite reasons why: We have surprise costs (leak, tax bill, legal, negative life events, etc.), my birthday, anniversary, holiday, founders discount, damaged goods, beta testers, spoil our local community, new program, new flavors/sizes/formula, you're only limited by your creativity and the bad (or good things) that happen to you.

If you say you will only offer *this* discount once and never again, stay true to it. To keep flexibility, you can always change what is included in your offer so that you can still sell at this "rate" again, just don't sell the same thing you made available for "one-time only"— *twice*. To be clear, businesses test price points all the time. You just want to make sure you do not offer two different prices to two different people *at the same time for the same thing*.

You can offer a Lifetime Discount on one thing so long as they buy another at retail. If you have two or more services that are complementary, consider giving one at a steep forever founder's discount and make up the profit on the other. Fancy business people call this a "loss leader". For example, you could give an insane founder deal on "meal planning'" to attract boatloads of new customers…provided they pay retail for "meal prep services". In other words, you can use insane founder's discounts to *attract* leads then make your profits on the upsell. This often works better than two mid-priced offers or a generic 25% off the top of both.

If a customer wants to leave the program, remind them they'll lose the discount. This will save some customers from leaving.

If a customer wants to return after canceling a Lifetime Discount. First, don't give it back to them or you will lose credibility with everyone else. Second, offer them a downsell that meets the same price but has different features. I've found this to work best for people who are price sensitive.

The Bigger The Head, The Longer The Tail

Bonus: The upsell comes built in. As soon as they like the product, make the original offer again. If they pay the difference of their down payment, they can lock in lower monthly payments. You can also offer to lock in this lower rate for life. *"If you put down $XXX we'll let you permanently buy down your monthly rate to $X, and keep it for life."* This helps get more cash and a stickier customer.

When I was being mentored by John, the tanning empire king, he used to joke, "I just want $1 from everyone in the world." He had built a massive low-price monthly recurring tanning chain in Southern California. He taught me a lot about the subscription revenue business. I'm very grateful for the wisdom he would share over our long car rides. One of the biggest lessons I learned came when he was explaining how initiation fees worked. I didn't even know they were "a thing".

"So guess which membership has the longest stick rate?" John asked, to lay context for his explanation of initiation fees.

"The cheapest one?" I guessed, waiting to hear the answer.

"The one where they pay the most up front," he replied, grinning sheepishly.

I didn't understand. He could tell I didn't get it and continued, "If I get someone to pay $100 to sign up, and lower their rate from $18 to $10/mo, I'm never losing that person. They'll even call me before their card changes to make sure they get to keep that lower rate. So they basically 'buy' a lower rate, but by doing that, they extend how long they stay by a ton. The more you can get people to commit up front the longer they'll stick."

Being a little slow on the uptake, the thought that *the bigger the head, the longer the tail* came to my mind, and I wrote a note in my phone for later so I wouldn't forget. That's when I learned the power of initiation fees for continuity.

Another way to spin this same concept is to waive a hefty initiation fee *if* they commit to a longer duration of time. An example would be saying, "You have two options: you can either pay $100 today, then go into month-to-month at $10/mo, cancel whenever you like, *or* you can start today for $10 and commit to the year. If you commit to the year, I'll waive the $100 initiation fee."

This may seem to fly in the face of the above point because you think everyone would just take the lower fee and save the $100…but wait. If they for some reason try, and then cancel before the duration of their contract, you say, "Absolutely, no problem. All we have to do is switch you over to the month-to-month plan. Just cover the initiation fee of $100 that we waived, and we'll get you switched right over." So by having this bigger "head," you get a longer stick on the back end as many will choose to just finish out their contract than pay the steep fee.

The reason getting people to pay more up front gets them to stay longer is a psychological phenomenon called the "Sunk Cost Fallacy". Basically, people will disproportionately continue to invest in a choice in which they've already invested time or money, even if it no longer makes sense. You hear it in statements like, "we've already come this far," "we've already put in so much time," and "we might as well just finish it."

This psychological principle is dangerous. If you don't recognize it in yourself, you will expose yourself to far more risk than you otherwise should, and you will stick with things longer than you would otherwise (simply because you already have). This goes for partnerships, memberships, investments, gambling, and so much more.

So getting more up front capitalizes on this psychological bias. But initiation fees don't just work on one bias, they work on multiple. Let me give you a different example.

The Greater Up Front Payments Compared To The Scheduled Payments, The More Likely The Customer Will Complete Them. If I get paid $1,000 today then have five monthly payments of $100, I'll likely collect the next five payments. On the other hand, if I ask for $100 per month for five months, and $1,000 at the end, the likelihood that the last payment goes through is lower. We account for this risk by adding more to the up front payment, creating a paid in full discount, or increasing the cost of ending their discount and reminding them of the cash they'll forfeit (the up front payment) and the price they'll lose (it'll be more expensive if you come back). We want to remind them of these things as close to the purchase or cancel as possible.

Summary Points

Know your numbers. Preserve your margins. Deliver a killer product. If you can do this, then lifetime discount customers will flock to your door and scale your business at a profit.

- Lifetime Discounts lead to stickier customers because they lose the discount if they stop.

- Lifetime Discount offers makes a product or service cheaper for a customer *as long as they stay on recurring payments.*

- Add urgency and scarcity to make the Lifetime Discount offer (or any offer!) more compelling.

- Use life events (both negative and positive) as reasons to offer a Lifetime Discount.

- If you offer a Lifetime Discount then you have a higher retail price.

- You can offer Lifetime Discounts in three ways: (%) off retail, ($) off retail, and fixed price.

- Make sure you have a healthy LTGP *after the discount.*

- This offer builds word of mouth because insane deals on great products get around fast.

Continuity Offer: Discount + One-Time Fee

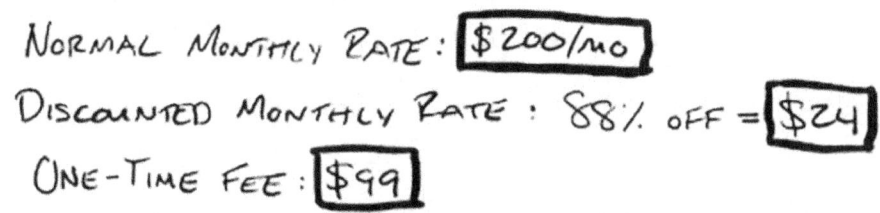

NORMAL MONTHLY RATE: **$200/mo**

DISCOUNTED MONTHLY RATE: 88% OFF = **$24**

ONE-TIME FEE: **$99**

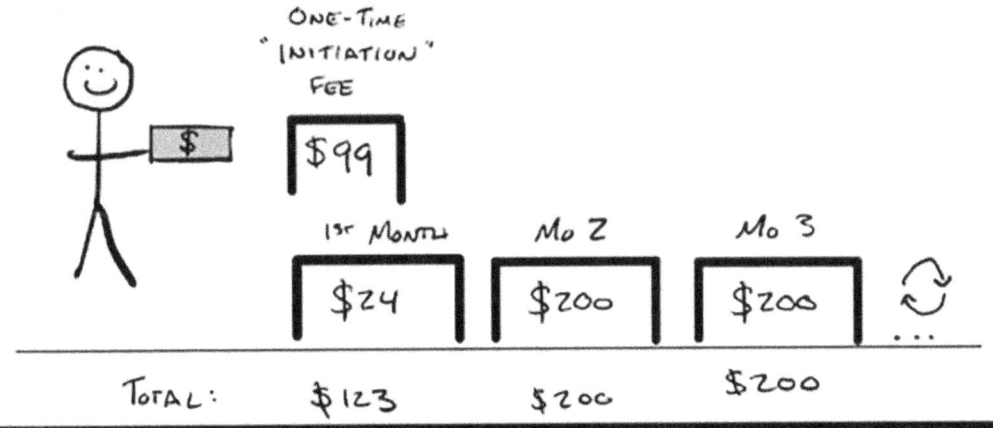

ONE-TIME "INITIATION" FEE

$99

	1ST MONTH	MO 2	MO 3	
	$24	$200	$200	...
TOTAL:	$123	$200	$200	

OFFER: OFFER X% OFF YOUR PRIMARY SERVICE THEN USE A ONE-TIME FEE. "WE DO THIS BECAUSE YOU'RE GOING TO REQUIRE A LOT MORE ATTENTION FROM US UP FRONT, BUT AFTER YOU UNDERSTAND HOW EVERYTHING WORKS, YOU WON'T NEED US, WHICH IS WHY YOU ONLY NEED TO PAY THIS ONCE."

OBJECTIVE:
1. LIQUIDATE ACQUISITION COST
2. PAY SALESMAN COMMISSION
3. INCREASE BUY-IN OF CUSTOMER
4. COVER HIGHER COST OF "ONBOARDING" A NEW CLIENT

Spring 2015.

I was walking out the front door of my La Habra location. The sun baked the black asphalt of the empty parking lot. It was midday, before the afternoon rush would begin in a few hours. Before I could take a step towards my car, a man quickly approached me, almost out of nowhere.

"Hey are you the owner?"

I was a bit startled, but said, "Yeah."

Before I could ask what he wanted, he ploughed right into his pitch.

"My name is Owen. I'm a personal training manager of a gym that just went under across town. I've got a group of trainers that just want to sell PT packages. We do about $100,000 per month in personal training sales. We just need a facility to work out of."

"We don't really offer personal training here," I said, half-lying because I didn't like the guy's vibe. He didn't seem trustworthy. I started to turn my side to him to show I wasn't interested and began to make my way towards my car.

He realized he needed to change his approach. "I promise we're a self-sufficient team. I can see through the window that you guys have a lot of dead space even when your sessions are going on. We can just help you monetize that area. It'll cost you nothing. It's just upside."

"It'll cost me time and attention," I countered, "and most importantly, it'll cost me the goodwill I've accrued with my customer base."

"No no no. We won't even talk to your customers if you don't want us to. We'll go get our own leads and sell them. We just ask that you give them a discounted month up front. And we charge an enrollment fee, which I just give to my guy as commission for the sale. Whatever they can close for the fee is theirs. That's how we do it. It'll cost you nothing."

"I'll think it over."

After thinking it over, I decided I did not want a foreign group of trainers and salespeople that I hadn't vetted walking around my gym representing my company. But I did notice the offer structure he presented. A discount *plus* a fee. He had clearly seen success with it, that much I believed. And this was the first I'd heard of this monetization structure. It both attracted customers with the discount and liquidated commissions and acquisition costs through the fee.

Here's how it works.

Description

You charge a discounted rate for your first term or period of service. You then charge one or more additional fees that you have "made up," just like the Free with Fee structure. You can waive some and charge others, waive them all, or charge them all. It gives you a lot of offer flexibility, depending on the strength of the salesperson. This offer will tend to surprise fewer people since they already came in expecting to pay something, which is one of the key benefits of using Discounts over Free for this particular structure.

Examples

Any Recurring Service

Offer: 95% off First Month / $1,900 off First Month / First Month for $100

Monetization: They come in for the first month for $100, but still get charged a $1,900 setup fee. All in all, they get charged $2,000 and go straight into recurring. From a monetization perspective, they just got charged $2,000 their first month and each month thereafter.

Any Defined-End Service or Program

Offer: 88% First Month (Selling a 12 Week Program for $3,000)

Monetization: You say it costs $1,000/mo for three months, but you get 88% off your first month ($120) and we have a $1,000 setup fee. They end up paying $1,120 for their first month then continuing their next two payments of $1,000 each.

Details

The higher the one-time startup fee, the lower the churn. The higher the barrier to entry, so too becomes the higher the barrier to exit.

John told me that when his tanning empire had a $100 sign-up fee for a $10/mo membership price, the churn on those clients was next to nothing, whereas the clients who signed up for $19 down and $19/mo churned at a higher rate.

This means you can use these "made up fees" we've been talking about to actively decrease your churn and increase the investment of your prospects. This helps them and you in the long run. Everyone wins. When people pay, they pay attention.

This is *especially* important for services where you require something to be done by the customer—getting you information, filling out forms, showing up at certain times, making selections, changing behavior, etc. If you need someone to do something in order to be successful, then more times than not, it makes sense to charge a one-time startup fee of some kind to get them invested in the long run.

You can even have a massive disparity between setup and recurring fee. A good friend of mine who runs a multi-million dollar online weight loss coaching business charges $5,000 to start and only $267/mo thereafter. His average client lifespan is more than two years (compare that with the normal average fitness client who stays four months). This large up front sum gets the client invested in the process and makes leaving almost insane.

And you guessed it. If they leave and want to come back, they have to pay it again. So this keeps people committed, especially when they have to do part of the work to achieve the result you sold them on (whatever that may be).

Note: Be clear about what the "reason" for the one-time fee is (even though it's made up). This should not be a fee taken lightly. It's also something that you should bring up with any and every customer. You are doing the work, so you might as well let them know exactly what you are going to be doing for them.

So here are the four steps to creating your one-time fee(s):

1) Pick Your Fee Name

2) Pick Your Fee Price

3) Pick Your "Reason Why"

4) Start Charging It, Discounting It, Or Waiving It

Summary Points

This play is incredibly flexible. You can use it in almost any type of business. The big discount can attract a lot of interest. These fees will help you offset the acquisition costs of marketing and sales. It also works very well with recurring or defined-end programs. And, in general, the larger the one-time fee up front, the higher the stick rate. Not only does this help you make money on the front end, it can dramatically enhance the lifetime value of the customer. These fees are also really good to think through, even if you don't plan on using this monetization structure, as they can provide additional revenue streams for your business. There are lots of things you're doing as a business owner, you might as well get credit for it. Waiving made-up fees can also help you generate more goodwill than signing someone up. You can also leave these fees to the discretion of the salesperson to help them "sweeten" the deal for someone on the edge. Unlimited uses here.

SECTION D: EXPANDED EMPLOYEES CHAPTER

"If you want to go fast, go alone. If you want to go far, go together" - African Proverb

Lost Chapter Author Note: ***Obviously there is an employee chapter in my $100M Leads book. I ended up cutting over half of it because I thought the chapter got too long and it started to creep into operations. But, enjoy the frameworks inside. They've been useful for me to transfer skills to teammates which is what you need to ultimately scale.***

June 2021.

The new sales director piped up, "I know we came in under our goal again, but I don't think we need to change anything, we'll hit it this quarter."

Eyes darted around the room and looked in every direction but mine. The silence was long enough for the executive assistant to mark the topic covered and move on. No wonder we missed our cold outreach goal for the second quarter in a row…nobody challenged the failure. *What, so now we think the third time's a charm?*

"Wait." I said. Now *everyone* looked in my direction. "I'd like to know why we didn't hit this two quarters in a row. I know we can sell—so if we want to make more sales with cold outreach, then we *do* more cold outreach. What's the issue?"

"We lose a rep every four weeks," the sales director said. *Aha.*

"Ok…Why is our churn so high?"

"I was wondering the same thing, but HR says we're actually below industry average churn for this position." He continued, "But, by the time we hire and onboard one, another churns out."

I saw the HR Director nodding in agreement. *Getting warmer.*

"OK, so the issue is hiring," I said. "So, what's the hiring situation look like?"

"We hire one out of every four candidates HR pushes to us."

"So if they churn out as fast as we hire them, and you only hire one out of every four, that means you only get like one candidate a week?"

"Yeah, about that." *Almost there.*

"Gotcha." Now I looked at the HR Director. "What's the screening situation look like?"

"We get one qualified candidate per ten screening interviews, give or take," she said.

"So it takes *forty* interviews to get a single, low-skill, frontline worker?"

"I guess so." *Bingo.*

"Alright, we need to change things up." I said. "We're bottlenecked at the one-on-one screening. Start interviewing in groups and look for crazies there. Push everyone else with a good work ethic and basic social skills over to sales. We can teach the rest. Agreed?" The team nodded.

Within six weeks, hiring outpaced churn. Our cold outreach sales increased in lockstep. By the end of the quarter, cold outreach sales had doubled, and made up more than half our total sales.

The issue wasn't our cold outreach method, skills, or offer at all. We just didn't have enough people *doing* cold outreach.

***

If you use the methods described in *$100M Leads*, you will see more engaged leads flow into your business. More engaged leads means more customers. But as you grow, so does your workload. In due time, it will take more work than any single person can handle. And you can solve the problem of too much work for one person *by having more people work*. In short, to advertise more, you'll need more workers. And this chapter will show you how employees work, why they make you wealthy, how to get them, and the method I use to turn them into lead-getters.

How Employees Work

Lead-getting employees are people working in your business that you train to get you leads. They get you leads the exact same way you got your own leads in the beginning. They can run ads, they can make and post content, and they can do outreach. They can do any advertising *you train them to do*. So more lead-getting employees means more engaged leads for your business. It also means less work *you* have to do to get the leads. More leads and less work? Sign me up! But wait… Not so fast…

Don't get me wrong—*employees take work.* They just take less time and work than doing everything on your own. In my experience, if you trade forty hours of doing for four hours of managing, you work thirty-six hours less. Brilliant. And the best part is, you can make that trade over and over. You can swap 200 hours of work per week for twenty hours of management. Then, you trade the twenty hours of managing for a manager, who costs you four hours per week to lead. What remains is four hours of work for 200 hours of lead-getting. Boom.

<u>Bottom Line</u>: Employees make a fully functioning enterprise that grows *without you*.

Why Employees Make You Wealthy

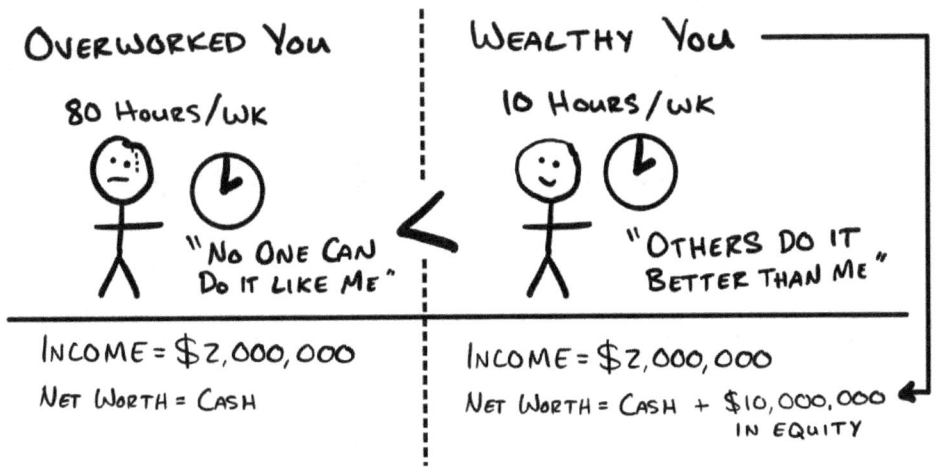

For your business to run without you, other people need to run it.

<u>Scenario #1</u>: Imagine you have a business that makes $5,000,000 per year in revenue and $2,000,000 in profit. And, to make that profit, you have to work around the clock. In this situation, you basically have a high-paying job. But let's say you're OK with working all hours and knowing your business would burn down if you took a vacation. Vacations are for losers anyways (kidding *cough* sort of...). We still have another important thing to look at...

Sure, you make a bit of money, but your business *isn't worth much*. If the business only makes money with you in it, then it's a *bad investment for anyone else*. That may not sound like a big deal right now, but let's consider an alternative.

<u>Scenario #2</u>: Your business makes the same $5,000,000 in revenue and $2,000,000 in profit. But there's one big difference: The business runs *without you*. This does two very cool things. One, it turns what used to be a risky job into a valuable asset. And two, it makes you *much* wealthier. Here's how:

First, you get your time back, so you can use that time to invest in your business, buy other businesses, or take your stinkin' vacations. Second, you become much wealthier because your business is now *worth something to someone else*. You turned a *liability* that relied on you into an *asset* you can rely on.

If you have an asset that makes millions of dollars *without you* then that means somebody else could use it to make millions of dollars *without them*. In other words, your business is now a *good investment*. Then investors looking for assets, like Acquisition.com for instance, would buy some or all of it from you. And your $2,000,000 in profit per year, especially if it's climbing, could easily be worth $10,000,000+, *right now*. So your business went from having almost *zero* value to having $10,000,000 of value.

You get rich from what you make. You become wealthy from what you own. And it took me years to realize this because not *that* long ago…

Everything I Thought I Knew About Employees Was Wrong

Have you ever heard…

> *If you want it done right, you gotta do it yourself.*
>
> *No one can do it like I do it.*
>
> *Nobody can replace me.*

I have. I said all that stuff. I lived all that stuff. For years, every time I hired somebody, I would compare what they could do to what I could do. In my head, I felt like it was "me against them". To somehow prove I was the more "able" one. With my own team! And this belief, this way of "leading" people, never made me more money.

For business—"nobody can do it but me" and "if you want something done right you gotta do it yourself" aren't facts…they're false. Somebody did similar stuff before you were around. And somebody will continue doing some version of it after you're gone. In one way or another, everyone is replaceable. It might be by multiple people, technology, or later in time, but *everyone* can be replaced. My suggestion: replace yourself as soon as you can. Then, you can make yourself useful somewhere else. Many other people figured this out. And so can you.

In the early days, whenever I started a business, I could do stuff better than the people I hired. My entire workforce always ended up looking like a ragtag group of misfits who could *kind of* do *one* of the many things I could do. This got me up and running at first, but I fell into the trap of believing I was better than everyone else. I would go back and forth between gloating because I was better than them and complaining because they weren't as good as me. And for whatever reason, it never occurred to me *I was the one* who hired and trained them. Who was I kidding? The reality was twofold: First, I didn't have the skills to train or lead a team properly. Second, I was too poor, and then (when I had a little money) too cheap to hire anyone better. In other words, it was <u>*my*</u> fault they sucked. Oops.

The more I tried to outcompete my employees, the more distracted I became, and the worse my business got. Sure, maybe I could do *anything* better than *any* of my employees. But… I couldn't do *everything* better than *all* my employees. And when I finally realized this, I started adopting better beliefs about talent:

> *If you want it done right, get someone to spend all their time doing it.*

> *If I can do it, someone else can do it better.*

> *Everyone is replaceable, especially me.*

These new beliefs about talent not only made a much healthier culture in my businesses but also came with very profitable side effects. Trusting my employees to succeed made *my* time and attention *far* more valuable. If somebody else can do it, why would I? If somebody else could train them, why would I? If I could learn other stuff to grow the business while my team held the fort down, it made *way* more sense to do that. So let's do that.

How Getting Employees Works: The Five Lead Stages

There are five stages a lead goes through before becoming a customer. Each lead stage is a reaction to something your business does. This means the way you run your business turns leads into customers or not. And this is good. Better yours than someone else's!

The lead stages are self-explanatory:

Uncontacted → Contacted → Engaged → Qualified → Sold

ACQUISITION CHANNEL: LEAD STAGES

STRANGER ⟶ CUSTOMER

	UNCONTACTED	CONTACTED	ENGAGED	QUALIFIED	SOLD
ACTION	No Activity	Advertise	Incentivize (OFFER!)	Nurture ?⤳X ·⤳✓	Sell ? ⟶ $
REACTION	Ignorant	See/Hear	Engage	Qualify ✓✓✓	Buy $ ⟶

Let's walk through each:

1) Leads start out *uncontacted.* You have done nothing they can react to yet.

   Action: You advertise to them.

2) Leads go from *uncontacted* to *contacted* when you get their attention.

   Next Action: You incentivize them to engage with your lead magnet or offer.

3) Leads go from *contacted* to *engaged* when they show interest in your lead magnet or offer.

   Next Action: You qualify them by learning their problems and money situation.

4) Leads go from *engaged* to *qualified* if they have a problem you solve and money to solve it.

   Next Action: You sell them by making an offer you'll fulfill in exchange for money.

5) Leads go from *qualified* to *sold* when they give you money in exchange for what you offer.

If you're wondering why I bring the lead stages up now, this far in, it's because *they have the most value now*, this far in. Again, for years, I struggled to build good teams for my businesses. I would either hire anybody I could find and throw them to the wolves. Or, I would cross my fingers hoping one of my best customers would work for me. Sure, this got me (and will get you) off the ground. But it's a far cry from what it takes to build a *$100M Leads* machine. When that finally sunk in, I realized something…

Getting new employees was the same as getting new customers. We just describe it with different words. This blew my mind when I stumbled on it. And once I looked at it this way, my hiring problems pretty much solved themselves. Let's break it down together.

INTERNAL LEAD STAGES

STRANGER ⟶ EMPLOYEE

	UNCONTACTED	CONTACTED	ENGAGED	INTERVIEWED	HIRED
ACTION	No Activity	Advertise ◁))	Incentivize (Offer!)	Nurture ?↗x ↘✓	Job Offer ? → $
REACTION	Ignorant ∅	See/Hear 👁	Engage 👆	Qualify ✓✓✓	Accept $ →

Line up the actions to get employees with the actions to get customers and they fit like a glove.

Think about it this way—you have two types of customers: The customers who pay you and the customers you pay—your employees.

And the reason is this—humans are humans. The process of getting attention is the same. The process of helping make decisions is the same. *I just used different words to describe the same thing.*

How To Get Them: The Internal Core Four

Remember the Core Four (warm outreach, cold outreach, paid ads, posting content) from *$100M Leads?* Well, they work for getting employees too. Imagine that. By changing the frame from "letting potential customers know about your stuff" to "letting potential employees know about your stuff" it *immediately* turns into something you already know how to do. But some people also have the opposite problem—they already know how to get employees just fine but still struggle to get customers. *They are just people you let know about your stuff.* You do the same thing!

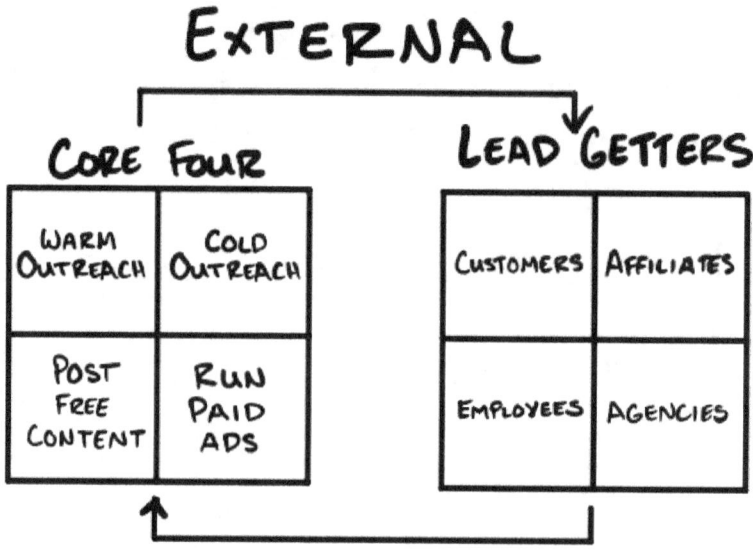

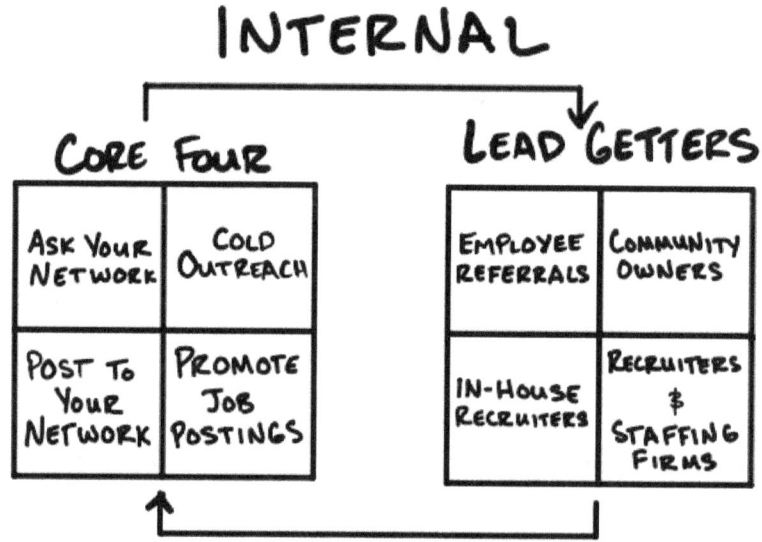

It's the same exact stuff! Isn't that cool?

Customers → Employees

Warm Outreach→Asking Your Network

Cold Outreach→ Recruiting

Post Content→Posting Job Openings

Paid Ads→Promoting Job Postings

Customer Referrals→Employee Referrals

Affiliates→ Associations, Guilds, Listservs etc.

Agencies→ Staffing firms, etc.

Employees→Employees (unchanged)

The ways you get employee leads and their lead getters have equivalents to the ways you get customer leads and *their* lead getters. So when you need to get new talent, you just advertise to get it. And when you need more, you do more. And like creating a reliable process to get customers, you can also create a reliable process of getting employees.

How To Get Employees To Get You Leads

Now you hire someone who costs you money every month. Great. Let's make sure you make it back, *and some* ASAP.

Note—some people looking for work will already know how to get leads. Those people are awesome. You can also count on them to cost more. And if you're starting out, you may not be able to afford them. So, your next best option is to train them. Thankfully, you have an entire book of lead-getting at your fingertips (*$100M Leads*). So the next step is training your employees on how <u>you</u> do those lead-getting activities. I think about and actually approach training with this 3Ds mental model: *Document, Demonstrate, Duplicate.* Here's how it works.

Step One—Document: <u>*You make a checklist.*</u> You already know how to do the thing. Now you just need to write down the steps exactly as you do it. You can also have other trusted observers watch you and document what you do. Bonus points if you record yourself doing the thing multiple ways and in multiple shifts. This way, you can watch yourself *as an observer* rather than breaking your flow by pausing to take notes while you go. Once you've got everything put into the checklist, bust it out on your next work block and *only* follow those steps. Can you do an A+ job *only* following *your* directions *exactly*? If you can, you have the <u>first draft</u> of your checklist for the job.

Step Two—Demonstrate: <u>*You do it in front of them.*</u> Just like the agency owner taught me how to run Facebook ads. You sit down and walk them through the checklist step by step. This may take a while depending on how many steps it takes to complete the thing. If they stop you, or slow you down, to understand something, adjust your checklist for that. Now you have the <u>second draft</u> ready for them to try.

Step Three—Duplicate: <u>*They do it in front of you.*</u> Now it's their turn. They follow the same checklist you followed. Except this time, they're the one doing, and you're the one observing. We just want them to *duplicate* what we did. So if the checklist is right, the outcome will be the same. And if the checklist is off—you'll find out fast! Fix your checklist until it's right. Then, have them follow it until they get it right. And once they nail it, you now have a bonafide lead-getter on your payroll. Congratulations!

After you train your first few employees this way, you'll have worked out the kinks for that job and it's pretty smooth sailing from there. (At least the training part anyways). Think about it this way, if you vanished tomorrow, could a stranger get the results you get if they only followed your checklist? That's the level of clarity to shoot for.

<u>Some helpful notes on training</u>:

- A helpful way to look at this training style is: *If they get it wrong or get confused then we got it wrong or made it confusing.* If we have to explain repeatedly what a step means then the step is too complicated. Or, more likely, we tried to put multiple steps into one.

- If they only appear to "get it" after a longish explanation or multiple demonstrations then, again, we've got some work to do. Business owners that ignore this run into chronic training problems. And, word to the wise, you can probably force an inferior checklist to work, but this turns into a *nightmare* when somebody else takes over your training for you.

- There is a difference between competence and performance. In other words, they can know exactly what to do and *not be that good at it yet*. If that's the case, then your instructions are fine and *they just need practice*. Using an analogy from the fitness world—think "slow then smooth then fast".

- *Focus on your employee's ability to follow directions more than whether they get the right result.* This is super important because if you train your employees to follow directions then…they will follow directions. And, if they follow directions and get the wrong result…*then you know it's the directions*. That's good. You have a lot more control over that.

- Every time they do a step successfully—*let them know they did it right*. And if they respond to praise, praise them! And if they goof, that's OK too. That's what training is for. Don't take over for them when they mess up—simply pause, take a step back, and let them try it again. Fast feedback cycles to get people to learn *faster*.

- If they follow your directions *exactly* and get the wrong result—still praise them for following the directions. Praise them, then make the corrections to your checklist on the spot.

- Avoid punishment or penalties of any type for doing stuff wrong during training. As a rule of thumb—reward the good stuff you want them to do more of and they'll do more of it. Learning a new skill is punishing enough, we don't need to add to it.

- If they mess up multiple steps, only focus on fixing one step at a time. Give one piece of feedback at a time. And remind them and give feedback on it until they get it right. Then move to the next step. It's very hard to change multiple things at the same time *when you've never done something before.*

Keep Your Employees Getting You Leads—The Performance Diamond

PERFORMANCE DIAMOND

①
COMMUNICATION

②
TRAINING ↔ PERFORMANCE ↔ ③
MOTIVATION

④
CIRCUMSTANCES

They do it on their own, with frequent check-ins.

Now that they know how to do it, we have to *keep* them doing it. Here's how. Depending on the business, I or my managers meet with each lead-getting employee six to 11 times per week. I know it sounds ridiculous, but it's really not.

I schedule one 30 to 45 minute meeting per week for coaching, feedback, and praising success. The other times are *short group meetings that only last a few minutes.* We call them "daily huddles"—and all my lead-getting employees have them. We have one at the beginning of each shift to discuss expectations and goals. Then, we have one at the end of each shift so they can report on them. I get an opportunity to praise and reward their efforts *daily.* This creates faster feedback cycles for building skills *and* morale.

If necessary, we take an extra few minutes to troubleshoot and answer questions that came up during the shift. If these problems or questions keep coming up, I add those to my training checklist for the next person I hire. Over time, you can have a team leader or manager take over the huddles and, eventually, the one-on-ones. Provided their performance stays the same or improves, you've successfully integrated the skill. You made it so they can feed their family for the rest of their lives. I know of few (if any) more noble callings.

Troubleshooting: What to do if they stop doing a good job? In my experience, there are four reasons employee performance drops. Here's how we solve for them.

1) **Communication—Employees don't know THAT we want them to do it.** If an employee didn't know we wanted them to do something then we didn't communicate that we wanted it done properly. Even if *we* think we did, their performance shows otherwise.

    Keep in mind—once we learn a skill, *we need to be reminded more than we need to be taught*. Remember, you are the chief accountability officer in the beginning and always. Afterall, it's your business—you are always accountable. So really, the only thing that changes is who you remind to do what. Even if it means you remind somebody to do their reminding!

    Here's what it sounds like when you have a communication problem:

    "I didn't know you wanted me to do that."

    "I didn't know you wanted me to do that <u>first</u>."

    "I've got too much work on my plate right now."

    Don't blow this off. It's so easy to point the finger and say "How can you not know your own job!?" But my business improved a lot when I actually believed them and started to point the finger at myself. So if I ever have this problem, I have them summarize the where, when, and how much they're supposed to perform their tasks. In essence, I have them describe their job and priorities back to me. If we think different stuff, then I know I need to do a better job at making things clear.

    And you may be surprised—they may still be working on that top priority thing you asked them to do a…few hours earlier (ha).

2) **Training—Employees don't know HOW to do it.** Assuming employees know *that* you want them to do it, they forgot how or were never taught! We account for this with strong initial training (onboarding) and regular practice of the basics to maintain and improve competence (daily huddles).

Here's what a training problem sounds like:

"I don't know how to do that."

"I didn't know you wanted me to do it <u>that way</u>."

Similar to number one—don't blow this off. Again, it's easy to point a finger and say "I already taught you how to do this! Seriously?"—But really…did we? How do we *really* know that?

Often, we think we taught somebody something if we ask "do you understand this?" and they say "yes". But even more often *they are just conditioned to say "yes" out of fear of saying "no"*. So, instead of asking if they understand and then holding it against them later—just have them *show* you. Let them demonstrate the checklist like they did in training. And treat them as you would anyone else learning for the first time, with patience, understanding, and fast useful feedback.

3) **Motivation—Employees don't WANT to do it.** Assuming they know *that* you want them to do it, and *how* to do it, they might not want to do it. And people don't want to do things for three main reasons:

   o "Reward" comes at: the wrong time, wrong frequency, wrong intensity, or the wrong source

   o They have an aversion to: the work itself, environment, leadership, coworkers, consumers

   o They have events or other lifestyle stuff *outside work* killing their performance

      i) Positive Event Example: Newborn baby, wedding

      ii) Negative Event Example: Death in family, break-up/divorce

      iii) Lifestyle Examples: Not sleeping enough, too much alcohol, getting sick, other medical conditions

Solving it comes from asking questions with these three levers in mind. Are you not rewarding them correctly? If so—increase frequency, intensity, or change *who* is doing the rewarding. Is there something about the workplace that makes it demotivating? This can give us insights to more systemic issues. Or, often, is there something we can only discover by asking them what's eating their attention outside of work? So, we ask open-ended questions to see what they'll share. Beyond having a genuine heart to help, sometimes you just gotta let people figure out their own stuff *on their dime rather than yours*.

Pro Tip: The Best Diamond Hard Feedback Question

If an employee's performance has been dropping for a little while (a week or two), here's a line I stole from Leila (like most of my good ideas). Use it in your next weekly one-on-one:

"Over the last (length of time) your (task performance) has changed from the norm.

What do you think has gotten in the way and how can I help?"

This question sets the stage for a collaborative problem-solving conversation rather than a character-blaming one. Swipe it if you like it.

---

4) **Circumstances—Something is stopping them**. I feel like I need to give you rapid examples of this. Unfortunately, this is more common than you think. In short—business owners (me included) tend to expect employees to solve problems we should have prevented to begin with!

   o   "Go grill the burgers"→ "I can't. We're out of beef."

   o   "Go edit videos"→ "I can't. My internet is too slow to download the file."

   o   "Go make calls"→ "I can't. The phone broke."

Understand the difference between them "making excuses" and making their life legitimately difficult. Assuming good communication, training, and motivation—all three of the above, *something* is stopping them. These are some of the easiest to fix, but you have to ask to find out. And as silly as what they're gonna say may sound—*don't shoot the messenger*.

This is the performance diamond I use for diagnosing performance problems. If I approach performance with that perspective it goes a long way to figuring out whether it's truly the employee's problem or, more often, something I messed up along the way. I say this because, most times, both you *and* them want them to succeed. So once you figure out what the problem is, fix it—and improved performance will likely follow.

Now we know how to get them and keep them advertising, the question that remains is, how well are we doing?

How to Calculate Returns From Lead-Getting Employees

Excluding the cost of running paid ads, the cost of advertising (outreach, content, etc.) with employees is almost entirely based on the amount of money you pay them to do it. We simplify this by just comparing how much money we spend on payroll to how much money the engaged leads they get bring in:

- Total Payroll / Total Engaged Leads = Cost per engaged lead.

    o Ex: $100,000 / 1,000 leads = $100 per engaged lead

- If one out of 10 of the engaged leads become customers then our CAC is $1,000

    o ($100 per engaged lead) x (10 engaged leads per customer) = $1,000 CAC

- If each customer has an LTGP of $4,000 then you have an LTGP : CAC of 4:1

    o ($4,000 LTGP) / ($1,000 CAC) = 4:1

For example: at the time of this writing, I get about 30,000 engaged leads per month at Acquistion.com. I run no paid ads, and do no outreach. But the team responsible for creating the content that generates that interest is about $100,000 per month. This means, it costs me roughly $3.33 per engaged lead ($100,000 / 30,000 leads) in payroll to generate them. We make much more than $3.33 per lead, so we're profitable. You can apply the same math to whatever advertising method you use.

How To Know Which Employees To Focus On To Maximize Returns

Like we learned in the Run Paid Ads Part II Chapter of *$100M Leads*—if your cost to get a customer is within 3x industry average then you're doing *good enough*. From there, you focus on bumping up your LTGP.

If your CAC is more than 3x industry average then you have a sales problem or an advertising problem. We diagnose this with a single question:

Do my engaged leads have the problem I solve and the money to spend?

- If no, then they're not qualified—that's an advertising problem.

- If yes, then they're qualified and:

    o They're buying but you don't have enough of them—advertising problem

    o They're qualified but not buying—sales problem.

Don't fire your sales guy if you've got advertising problems. And equally, don't fire your advertising employees if you've got a sales problem. That little question can help you identify which employees to focus on.

But fundamentally, you just need to figure out all *your* costs of getting a customer put together. And as long as they're at least one third of the profit you make over the lifetime, you're in good shape.

Conclusion

The goal of this chapter was to *shift your perspective*. It's your job to advertise and sell the vision of your company. You advertise it publicly *and* privately to employees *and* customers alike. That's the job. And once you get good at it, you become unstoppable.

I say this because I believe anyone can be taught to do "ground level" jobs for any business—advertising or otherwise. So who you pick is not as important as how you train the ones you do.

Like I've said throughout the book and will say again here—it doesn't take a genius to advertise. I'd even say it hurts it. We've got plenty more iron-wills than brainiacs anyways. Remember, this isn't about brains, it's about guts. And although some people might be born geniuses, *nobody* is born with an iron will (afterall, we all come out crybabies). All this to say, <u>having guts is a skill.</u> And that means *anyone* can have the guts *if they learn how.* So if you have an iron will, and as an entrepreneur you probably do, it won't take long for you to figure out that you got it from your life experiences. You can pass those experiences on as lessons to anyone who cares enough to listen. Then, they can stand on your shoulders and have a better chance at succeeding in life.

And—you can't really know anything anyway until you train them well and give them a fighting chance to succeed out in the field. Plus, for low-level jobs, you'll never have a shortage of labor. Get picky when you have to make massive investments in hyper-specific-multiple-six-figure-C-suite employees. Aka—"fancy employees".

I find at this current stage, it's actually a better use of time to hire and train anyone *willing*. Then, <u>when</u> you find winners, and with this method you will: treat them well, don't burn them out, and give them what they deserve.

144

In the land of overflowing leads, you'll need allies. Employees are among the most powerful of these allies. We talked about: how they make you wealthy, how they work, how getting them works, how to get them, how to get them getting you leads, how to keep them getting you leads, and how to know you're doing a good job. And once you've built a system for getting people who get you leads (doing the Core Four on your behalf), you just need to do more.

Maker or Manager?

How to turn time into money.

Lost Chapter Author Note**: *Time is the only resource we're given. The people who make the most money know how to trade it for the highest return. I wrote this on how I run my time. It's ruthlessly simple. It's also how we run the teams at Acquisition.com. And if you spend time, or manage people who do, this may be one of the most important things you ever read. Also, special thanks to Paul Graham who wrote about this concept 14 years ago. I borrowed the title in ode to it, and to expand upon it given my personal experience.*

A conversation happening everywhere around the world...

"You got time tomorrow morning?"

I look over to my empty calendar. *I suppose I could fit it in. But I was planning on taking a big chunk out of this project.*

"Uhh, yea I have some openings. How long you thinking?"

"Shouldn't take longer than an hour...say 10am?"

***

"Hey, I'm reaching out because John introduced us. Wanna grab a coffee sometime this week?"

I didn't think I needed anything at the moment. But I don't want to be rude.

"Yea, I think I can make time."

"Cool. Here's a great spot. ADDRESS. I'll meet you there, say 2pm?"

"Yea, that works. See you then."

The Two Types of Calendars

Both of these examples represent hundreds of millions of exchanges that happen every day. What you don't see is that to one person, this type of exchange costs ten times more than the other. Let me explain.

There are two very different ways to manage time for two very different types of work and workers. There are makers. And there are managers. I'll start with the one that most people are familiar with—managers—because this is how most of the world manages time…

Managers

Managers divide their time into small 30–60 minute blocks. This gives them between 10 to 20 chunks of work time per day. And each block often differs from the block before.

Their work often depends on meetings where they direct others. They collect data and report data to persuade, lead, train, encourage, and make other decisions. They talk to lots of different people and do many different kinds of tasks all day long. They have a pretty clear beginning and end to their work day. They basically work until their last calendar slot appointment.

For managers, an empty time slot is a lost opportunity. For that reason, they treat time like currency. And an empty time slot means "free" to fill with manager stuff. The only real cost for them to fill it is to coordinate with another person's empty time slot. On paper, since they "work" on meetings, a mutually filled slot <u>makes both people more productive</u>.

Their objective is to use up all the chunks in their day so they can maximize their time. Fair enough.

Makers

Makers, on the other hand, make up a much smaller number of workers (and shrinking!). *They actually make stuff*. And, they cannot "make" in small 30–60 minute blocks of time. And depending on what they make, it takes very large chunks of time, half-day or full-day blocks. Therefore, they have fewer of them. They may only have one to two chunks of time per day. And maybe 10 to 14 per week.

The work is often similar on the outside, especially day to day. For them, they have known work inputs (like keystrokes) but variable outputs (they often make something different every time). So seldom if ever do they have a task they can finish on any given 30-minute block. Their days typically have a similar start time but variable finish. They work "open to goal". In other words, they work until their quality output per unit time drops. *Their performance* decides when they're done for the day. And compared to managers, they have a more limited time they can work until they mentally exhaust themselves. And on a larger time horizon, the best makers only switch tasks when the project they work on is finished. So their work has relatively low urgency compared to the swashbuckling manager, but, at the same time, it can have the highest importance.

And, from the outside, a lot of their work may not look like work at all. An impressive percentage of the time doesn't go into labor people see. It often goes into *figuring out how to do the work people see*. They don't solve problems so they can work, solving *is* the work. They might get stuck for 45 minutes and then *bang*, it comes to them. Sometimes, problem-solving dry spells can last days. In my case, it took me upwards of six months just to figure out the table of contents for my second book. *That is the maker's work*. It means doing things, producing what nobody has produced before. At least not by anyone they have access to. And it also means producing in ways maybe nobody has gone about producing it. Otherwise, they would make something else.

Based on the immersive nature of their work, they incur a monumental cost of switching tasks. A meeting, even a short one, breaks the larger chunk into two smaller chunks, near unusable for maker's work. A whole work unit—poof! For example, a 10am meeting, even for 30 minutes, breaks their morning block into 2 hours and 1.5 hours. Not enough to get back into their immersive, deep, flow-dependent maker's work.

What's worse, when they do have something on the schedule, they "suffer" from something called the Zeigarnik effect. The Zeigarnik effect states that you will tend to remember open loops better than closed loops. Normally, this is a good thing. Like managers for instance, it helps them remember the stuff they have to do during the day. But for a maker, it's a mind-parasite. For them, the open loops and pending tasks eat up attention, disrupt immersion, and destroy a maker's productivity. Even if you know something happens in the afternoon, you know you must limit your morning work. You have to pay attention to make sure you end on time. Never mind the intrusive thoughts interrupting your day… now you must *also* watch the clock at a regular interval which interrupts the work you do leading up to the meeting. And at some point, you begin to think about what needs to be covered in the meeting, wholly removing the maker from their project at hand.

Makers get work done **outside** of meetings. <u>To a maker, an empty calendar means full productivity</u>. For makers, unless they have the luxury of working in a bomb shelter, it's easier to work when other people don't (early morning and late evening). This limits interruptions. But it also drastically inflates the amount of time they spend on their jobs (versus the time they spend working!). They "clock in" during the day, only to be interrupted all day, then finally start working when everyone else stops!

Their objective is to maximize the blank space on their calendar so they can have as many large uninterrupted chunks of time as possible.

The Problem

Makers and managers can both exist at the same time. Problems occur when they try to work together. When a manager tries to work with a maker, not knowing how makers work, it leads to productivity disasters. Since the relative time slot for the manager costs so little, *and* makes the manager more productive, they assume, and for good reason, it's also true for the maker. "It's just 30 minutes, and you've got the free time, what's the big deal?" But it couldn't be further from the truth. It costs makers 10x more. A short meeting costs one measly work unit for the manager…and a giant work unit for the maker.

What's worse, if a manager asks a maker to block time, the maker has two terrible outcomes. First, they either offend the manager (and incur other risks) by declining the invitation. Oftentimes this damages the relationship or decreases the likelihood of collaboration in the future (which they may need). Or they accept, and take an unreasonably high cost for a meeting that often yields…nothing.

Managers often assume that makers can work like they do, *on demand*. But this confuses the nature of managerial work and maker's work. And given the fact most people work on manager's schedules, it leads to huge losses in productivity and very late nights or early mornings for the maker who must accommodate everyone else's schedules—mostly out of fear and politeness.

This means managers often prevent the work they check in on! And when this happens (often), both parties lose. The manager takes a hit because the maker takes the hit. But this creates a trap. The worse the maker's performance gets *the more the manager tries to keep tabs on them!* Lose-lose.

Unfortunately, this is how most of the world works. But there is a better way...

The Solution

We attack the problem on three fronts. To the manager, to the makers, and to the organization.

To the managers:

Step 1: Understand both costs you put on a maker.

First, the cost of coordinating times while they work destroys their productivity. And once you have a time set aside, understand that the time itself eats up an entire work block. Know the difference between your work and a maker's work. When you ask for a meeting, it costs them ten times more. You use up one of their 10 slots per week. I'm not telling you to not...meet your makers. Just that if you want your organization to be more productive, <u>understand the costs of your requests</u>. And when you make them, **be sure it is worth it.**

Step 2: Understand the value of the maker's "no".

If a maker declines a meeting, do not take offense. See it as them trying to keep their larger commitment to you and others—to get the meaningful project done.

To the makers:

Step 1: Good managers WANT TO HELP YOU. **Let them.**

Part of that responsibility lies on you to make managers aware of the differences between your work and schedules. Send this piece of content to them to *help them help you.* And yes, you will have to take meetings that eat your entire day sometimes. When that happens, fight fire with fire—*swap to a manager's calendar style.*

All makers have *some* administrative tasks to do. And since you've lost the chunk anyway, you can get some good feedback, serious wins, and other benefits by just dedicating the entire chunk to as many meetings and other administrative tasks as you can. That way, you can save other time blocks in the future from being made unusable.

Step 2: Make meeting blocks. And stick to them.

In addition, you can have standard "meeting" times where you accept these. And you must defend these. It's rare that a meeting is truly urgent. See if you can push them off to the designated blocks you set aside ahead of time. Make this time available to anyone who meets with you on a regular basis, and to people who ask to meet spur of the moment.

Since I'm an entrepreneur, I like to dedicate the first half of the day to doing maker's work and then the second half for manager's work. So people *can* meet with me pretty much every day…just *after* 1pm. Also, I schedule my meetings from back to front. This way, if somebody does get scheduled with me, it happens as late in the day as possible. This way, I can extend my maker's block a little bit. And even though the Zeigarnik effect takes hold, I can still get a little more done than I otherwise would have.

Pro Tip: How To Apply This As A Freelancer or Solopreneur

No one works on your calendar and you don't have anyone *on your team* to block for you. Expect no one to know how you work or why. When I had fewer means, I worked from 4am to 10am on my "maker" work, then tended to the usual fires of business during the day. This gave me nine work blocks. One per day during the week and two chunks each weekend day. You may have to adopt a schedule like this. With your real work happening before or after "the managers," interruptions cease. This got me through the early years. Beyond sharing this piece of content with everyone you work with, it may be a good in-between measure.

Step 3: Set expectations for slow responses during your maker's block.

People have an amazing ability to adapt if you tell them ahead of time. People really only get upset when you don't meet expectations. So—*change them!* Let everyone know this is how you work and this is when you will be responsive vs. not.

Step 4: Work when you say you work.

You only get to claim the title of "maker" if you make stuff. Otherwise, you're a fool and you make a fool out of anyone who calls themselves a maker.

If you have the luxury of people who respect your schedule, you owe it to them to make! If you waste time, you will confirm all their suspicions. They will think you never worked to begin with! And you damage your reputation *and the reputation of all other makers.* You make it less likely they will respect your work and your word in the future.

To the organizations:

Step 1: Consider mandated "quiet" time chunks.

During these, entire teams cannot message one another or meet. Either a chunk of time daily, or entire days of the week. It doesn't need to apply to the entire organization, only the ones where you have makers. Engineers. Developers. Copywriters. Builders. Presenters. Media editors. Etc.

Step 2: Spread this content to makers and managers alike so everyone can use the same language to describe this large source of waste…and prevent it!

My goal is to increase awareness of these two types of working styles and put words to something that plagued me for a long time. And hopefully, gives words to the makers out there, whose work moves the world. So that they can share this with the people who work with them, to hopefully explain how costly "got a min?" really is.

FREE GOODIES

My gift to you for being a part of this journey.

Kinda like the previews after the credits finish, if you're still with me, I wanted to give you a handful of goodies.

1) **If you want <u>free</u> training on all the concepts from the $100M Series** (*$100M Offers, $100M Leads, $100M Money Models*) just go to <u>acquisition.com/training</u>. My gift to you, enjoy.

2) **If your company is over $1M in EBITDA (profit)**, we'd love to help you scale. It brings so much pleasure to know companies have grown much bigger and faster than mine *because they avoided the mistakes I made*. If you want us to take a look under the hood and see if we can help go to **Acquisition.com**.

3) **If you want a job at Acquisition.com** or in one of our companies - we love hiring from #mozination. Our best returns come from investing in great people. Go to **Acquisition.com/careers/open-jobs**, and you can see all the available openings.

4) **If you learn more by listening**, my podcast at the time of this writing is top 5 in entrepreneurship and top 15 in business in the US. The crazy thing is, I started this podcast 90 days after I lost everything (the second time). So you can hear—day by day, month by month—my journey from $0 to $100M+. And everything I learned along the way—the whole thing is documented. I think that's pretty cool. You can find it by searching "Alex Hormozi" wherever you listen. Or, by going to **Acquisition.com/podcast**. I share useful and interesting stories, valuable lessons, and the essential mental models I rely on every day.

And last, thank you again. Please be one of those givers and **share this with other entrepreneurs by leaving a review**. It would mean the world to me. I'm sending you business building vibes from my desk. I spend a lot of time there, so it's a lot of vibes.

Be one of zero.

Alex Hormozi, Founder, Acquisition.com

www.ingramcontent.com/pod-product-compliance
Lightning Source LLC
Chambersburg PA
CBHW081535120626
46550CB00009B/2734